FLORIDA STATE S
2013 NATIONAL CHAMPIONS

UNCONQUERED!

OUR COVERAGE OF
A CHAMPIONSHIP TEAM

Tallahassee Democrat
Tallahassee.com
A GANNETT COMPANY

TALLAHASSEE DEMOCRAT
Tallahassee•com
A GANNETT COMPANY

Credits

Publisher: Julie Moreno/ @TDjamoreno

Executive Editor: Bob Gabordi/ @bgabordi

Multimedia News Editor: Rebeccah Lutz/ @RebeccahLutz

Sports Editor: Ira Schoffel/ @IraSchoffel

Assistant Sports Editor: Jim Henry/ @JimHenryTALLY

NoleSports.com Editor: Corey Clark/ @Corey_Clark

Multimedia reporter: Natalie Pierre/ @Natalie_Pierre

Photographers:

Glenn Beil/ @glennbeil

Mike Ewen/ @MEwenTD

Read more of the Tallahassee Democrat's coverage of Florida State University football:

NoleSports.com

@NoleSports

www.facebook.com/NoleSports

Peter J. Clark, Publisher
Molly Voorheis, Managing Editor
Katherine Grigsby, Layout & Design

© 2014 Tallahassee Democrat

All rights reserved. Except for use in a review, the reproduction or utilization of this work in any form or by any electronic, mechanical, or other means, now known or hereafter invented, including xerography, photocopying, and recording, and in any information storage or retrieval system, is forbidden without the written permission of the publisher.

ISBN: 978-1-940056-07-4 (PB)
ISBN: 978-1-940056-08-1 (HC)

Printed in the United States of America
KCI Sports Publishing   3340 Whiting Avenue, Suite 5   Stevens Point, WI 54481
Phone: 1-800-697-3756   Fax: 715-344-2668
www.kcisports.com

CONTENTS

FORWARD By CHARLIE WARD 4
PITTSBURGH 8
NEVADA 14
BETHUNE-COOKMAN 20
CHRISTIAN JONES & LAMARCUS JOYNER 24
BOSTON COLLEGE 28
MARYLAND 34
CLEMSON 40
TELVIN SMITH 46
NC STATE 50
BOBBY BOWDEN RETURNS 54
MIAMI 56
COACH JIMBO FISHER 62
WAKE FOREST 66
SYRACUSE 72
IDAHO 78
BRYAN STORK 82
FLORIDA 88
ACC CHAMPIONSHIP: DUKE 94
JAMEIS WINSTON 100
BCS CHAMPIONSHIP: AUBURN 106

FLORIDA STATE
FORWARD
BY CHARLIE WARD

Dear Seminole Nation,
Winning a national championship in 2013 was a great achievement for our dynamic football program and university.

Many people may not realize it, but the opportunity to win a championship is usually preceded by small wins throughout the course of the year. Whether it's players coming together in early August, players taking care of their academics, or players overcoming adversity, on or off the field, the small wins matter.

When it's all said and done, it's about going out and executing and playing at a high level, in this case, for 14 games. That is very, very difficult to do.

To win a national championship, a lot of things have to go right. However, the one constant theme throughout a championship team is the attitude of being one, the willingness to sacrifice individual goals for the betterment of the team.

That's what having the opportunity to win a national championship is all about, and makes this journey so special.

I was blessed with this opportunity in 1993. There were teams before us that had their opportunities, and those teams paved the way for us to be able to enjoy that special moment and be the first group (FSU football team) to win a national championship. And for Coach

Heisman Trophy winner Charlie Ward led FSU to the 1993 national title. *Photo: Democrat files*

Bobby Bowden to add that first title to his legacy, it was a great accomplishment for all of us.

What Coach Jimbo Fisher has done is remarkable. Many times when coaches follow legends, they have a difficult time, and programs have a tough time rebounding. But it all depends on the attitude of the head coach and players. And I think Coach Fisher took the right approach in making that happen and bringing the program together.

Of course, Coach Fisher will tell you, like any coach, it also doesn't hurt to have talented players, and a lot of them. There were many players on the 2013 team who have been with Coach Fisher since he was named head coach in 2010, and they provided great leadership. Two- and three-deep players (on depth chart) contributed in practice and in games. Coach Fisher established the mindset and attitude to win a national championship.

My advice to players is to enjoy the moment. Many times we get so caught up in the things around the moment that we somehow forget to actually enjoy it. Also, keep it in perspective and embrace it with humility, because this time will last only so long, and it will be time to move forward.

The greatest threat to success is previous success. Many times players think this is the way it's always going to be, and they don't put in the necessary work into making it happen again. Every year is different. You have to put in the time and effort to making your season special. Like this season.

People will ask if this team is the best in FSU history. That's fine with me. Every time a team and players win a championship – and we've been fortunate enough to win three national titles in 1993, 1999 and 2013 – it's their mark.

Charlie Ward, FSU's first Heisman Trophy winner and the quarterback who led FSU to its first National Championship, greets a friend during pregame ceremonies that honored that team in 2013. *Photo By: Mike Ewen/Democrat*

And what we all had in common was we came together as one and won a national championship. Regardless of what team is considered the best – I never understood that discussion anyway – I am so grateful that our alma mater will have another national championship under our belt.

Congratulations again to the 2013 team and our university. I hope you enjoy this book as you reflect on this wonderful accomplishment. Go Seminoles!

Charlie Ward
FSU, 1993

2013 NATIONAL CHAMPIONS

Head Coach Jimbo Fisher holds the championship trophy up after Florida State defeats Auburn 34-31 to take the BCS National Championship game on Jan. 6, 2014. The Florida State Seminoles used late-game heroics to take down the Auburn Tigers at the Rose Bowl in Pasadena, Calif. See game story coverage, page 106. *Photo By: Glenn Beil/Democrat*

HEINZ FIELD | SEPTEMBER 2, 2013

FLORIDA STATE   41
PITTSBURGH   13

A MAGICAL NIGHT TO REMEMBER

COMMON SENSE TELLS US TO GET A HOLD OF OURSELVES

BY IRA SCHOFFEL

PITTSBURGH, PA. — To remember this was one game. One night. One magical performance.

There's no way that anyone, let alone a redshirt freshman, can keep this up from week to week over the course of a 12-game season. So we need to settle down a little.

That's what common sense tells us.

But there was nothing common about what we witnessed here Monday night in the Seminoles' 41-13 victory at Heinz Field.

Against a Pitt team that returned eight starters from one of the nation's top 20 defenses, Jameis Winston was simply incredible. You know the stats – heck, we all know the stats. We might never forget the night we watched Winston complete 17 of 18 passes in the first half of his first career start. And then follow that up with an 8-of-9 performance in the second half.

In his first college football game.

On the road.

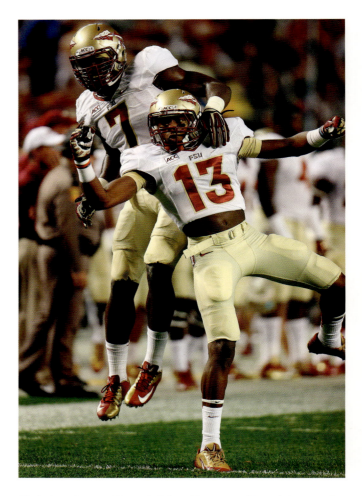

Christian Jones, 7, and Jalen Ramsey, 13, celebrate after Ramsey made an interception in the first quarter of play.
Photo By: Glenn Beil/Democrat

Kelvin Benjamin picks up yards after a catch as Florida State visits Heinz Field in Pittsburgh for the opening night of the 2013 football season against the Pittsburgh Panthers. *Photo By: Glenn Beil/Democrat*

Jameis Winston runs a keeper up the middle as Florida State visits Heinz Field in Pittsburgh for the opening night of the 2013 football season against the Pittsburgh Panthers. *Photo By: Glenn Beil/Democrat*

Quarterback Jameis Winston talks to the offense during a timeout as Florida State dominates the Pittsburgh Panthers at Heinz Field during the team's first game of the 2013 football season. *Photo By: Glenn Beil/Democrat*

But it wasn't the stats that grabbed your attention Monday night. It's the way Winston plays the position. The way he runs the offense. The way he stutter-steps in the pocket to set up a block. The way he feels pressure and releases the ball at just the right time.

It doesn't make sense for a freshman to play like that. Heck, during the past decade or so, we've seen some seniors that didn't play like that.

But that's kind of what Winston does.

Back in the spring, the common thinking was that Winston wouldn't factor into the quarterback competition as long as

Jalen Ramsey returns an interception in the first quarter as Florida State visits Heinz Field for the opening night of the 2013 football season against the Pittsburgh Panthers. *Photo By: Glenn Beil/Democrat*

he split time with baseball. Especially since he would be competing with two quarterbacks – junior Clint Trickett and sophomore Jacob Coker – with much more time in Jimbo Fisher's system.

Then he stole the show in the spring game, completing 12 of 15 passes for 205 yards and two touchdowns.

So for those of you scoring at home ... we have now watched Jameis Winston attempt 42 passes in a Florida State uniform (including that spring game). He has completed 37 of those 42, with six touchdowns and no interceptions.

And this kid was really in a quarterback battle with Jacob Coker until just last week?

That's not a knock on Coker. But if Winston looked anything like this in practice, it's difficult to imagine there was much of a decision to make.

The reality is Jimbo Fisher had to play it as slow as he could with Winston. The hype was already getting out of hand with him not being named the starter. Imagine if he had been promoted to No. 1 back in April?

But controlling the excitement is out of Fisher's hands now.

Florida State fans are clearly in love. Even former FSU players, like Danny Kanell and others, were on Twitter late Monday declaring that Winston might be the greatest quarterback in school history.

Common sense tells us that's insanely premature.

That there's no way this kid can keep this up for a month, let alone a career.

But there doesn't appear to be anything common about young Mr. Winston.

And for the Florida State Seminoles, uncommon might never have felt quite this good.

BOX SCORE

FLORIDA STATE 41, PITTSBURGH 13

FSU	7	21	6	7 —	41
PITT	7	3	3	0 —	13

First Quarter
PITT—Savage 4 pass to Street (Blewitt kick), 10:50.
FSU—Winston 24 pass to O'Leary (Aguayo kick), 4:11.

Second Quarter
FSU—Winston 1 pass to O'Leary (Aguayo kick), 13:41.
PITT—FG 28 Blewitt, 9:18.
FSU—Winston 5 run (Aguayo kick), 2:13.
FSU—Winston 23 pass to Greene (Aguayo kick), :38.

Third Quarter
FSU—FG 22 Aguayo, 11:24.
PITT—FG 39 Blewitt, 4:43.
FSU—FG 28 Aguayo, 1:12.

Fourth Quarter
FSU—Winston 10 pass to O'Leary (Aguayo kick), 9:32.
A—24,376.

	FSU	PITT
First downs	25	16
Rushes-yards	34-156	27-96
Passing	377	201
Comp-Att-Int	27-29-0	15-28-2
Return Yards	82	138
Punts-Avg.	2-37.0	3-54.3
Fumbles-Lost	0-0	0-0
Penalties-Yards	7-70	4-26
Time of Possession	35:08	25:52

DOAK CAMPBELL STADIUM | SEPTEMBER 14, 2013

FLORIDA STATE 62
NEVADA 7

'NOLES IN A LANDSLIDE
FSU OFFENSE PILES UP 377 RUSHING YARDS IN 62-7 WIN OVER NEVADA

BY COREY CLARK

Kenny Shaw couldn't believe what he was seeing.

There were fewer than six minutes left in the first half. Florida State had the ball at its own eight and was trailing visiting Nevada 7-3.

"We're a high-powered offense," the FSU senior receiver said.

"We don't need three points in the first half. We came together as a unit and said, 'Let's get it done.' We don't practice two hours a day to get three points in the first quarter (and a half) against Nevada."

The Seminoles got it done.

FSU (2-0) scored 59 points over the next 36 minutes, including a 31-point avalanche in the third quarter, to win 62-7 over the Wolf Pack on Saturday at Doak Campbell Stadium before a crowd of 73,847.

"It's like the snowball effect," redshirt freshman quarterback Jameis Winston said. "When it starts rolling, people keep picking up and we keep playing and we go higher."

Winston overcame a rough two-series stretch in the first half to finish 15 of 18 for 214 yards and two touchdowns. He also ran for another score.

FSU's James Wilder Jr. celebrates his second half touchdown run. *Photo By: Mike Ewen/Democrat*

Quarterback Jameis Winston airs it out in the first half. The FSU Seminoles took a hard-fought 17-7 lead into halftime against a tough Nevada Wolf Pack on a steamy day in Tallahassee. *Photo By: Mike Ewen/Democrat*

Ronald Darby tackles RB Chris Solomon with a little help from Christian Jones and Terrence Brooks in the game against the Nevada Wolf Pack. *Photo By: Steve Chase/Democrat*

After the first interception of his career set up Nevada's lone TD of the game, all Winston did was complete his final 13 passes for 184 yards and two touchdowns – to Shaw and Rashad Greene, respectively.

Through two games the freshman now has more touchdown passes (six) than he does incompletions (five).

"What I liked about it was he made a mistake and he didn't get gun shy," FSU coach Jimbo Fisher said. "He went right back into it and started making throws and making plays."

On the first touchdown, Shaw was actually being held by his facemask while he tried to make his cut toward the corner of the end zone. Winston still lobbed it in the perfect spot, and Shaw made a terrific grab to put the Seminoles ahead to stay.

FSU's Demonte McAllister (97) pressures Nevada quarterback Devin Combs in the first half. The FSU Seminoles took a hard-fought 17-7 lead into halftime against a tough Nevada Wolf Pack and then the Florida State rushing attack took over.
Photo By: Mike Ewen/Democrat

"When the throw came I was like, dang, that's a pretty good throw," Shaw said with a laugh. "(Even) slightly over and it would have been incomplete."

The other TD pass was also a thing of beauty, as Winston rifled it over the Nevada cornerback and Greene made a leaping catch at the goal line.

"It was a perfect pass," Greene said. "The defender didn't know it was there until the last minute. He put it right over the top of his head. That was a great throw. ... That's a perfect place for me to go up and get it."

Winston's two TD throws in the final 3:21 of the first half, both from 24 yards out, gave the Seminoles a 17-7 lead at halftime. And then the Florida State rushing attack took over.

The first three offensive plays of the second half for FSU were: Devonta Freeman 60-yard run, Freeman 6-yard TD run, Karlos Williams' 65-yard TD run.

Three rushes. All over the right side. For 131 yards and two scores. In the span of 3:13.

James Wilder Jr. watches as fellow running back Devonta Freeman dives over the goal line for a TD. Freeman carried the ball 9 times for 109 yards and a TD. The Seminoles defeated the Wolf Pack 62-7 to improve to 2-0 on the season.
Photo By: Steve Chase/Democrat

For the game FSU rushed for 377 yards, including a staggering 316 in the second half.

Williams (110 yards) and Freeman (109) combined for 219 rushing yards.

"That will make Coach (Rick) Trickett happy," right tackle Bobby Hart said. "It was just settling in. That's all it was. Just relaxing and doing what we needed to do."

"The second half we kind of changed our attitude," said right guard Ruben Carter, who started in place of the injured Tre Jackson.

Ten different players had at least one carry for the FSU offense on Saturday and eight caught at least one pass.

And though the FSU defense started slow on Saturday, having difficulty getting off the field against the Nevada offense, it rebounded with a fury in the second half.

It didn't help the normally high-powered Wolf Pack offense that it was forced to play third-string quarterback Tyler Stewart the final two quarters (starter Cody Fajardo sat out the game with a knee injury and backup Devin Combs injured his knee in the first half). But the Seminoles held Nevada to just 76 yards over its final nine drives.

"I feel like we played really well," said safety Terrence Brooks, who had a team-high six tackles. "But as for in the beginning, we hate doing that. We hate letting them getting the first blow and scoring on us like that. But it's good that we kept our composure and kept playing."

Florida State didn't have a sack on Saturday but forced a number of errant throws, and safety Tyler Hunter accounted for the team's lone turnover with a third-quarter interception.

"I was very proud of our defense," Fisher said.

"They did a great job on the passing game. They knocked the ball down, we got pressure on the quarterback ... we affected the quarterback. Got some shots on him. Our defense I thought played really well. Made some nice adjustments."

BOX SCORE

FLORIDA STATE 62, NEVADA 7

FSU	3	14	31	14 —	62
NEVADA	0	7	0	0 —	7

First Quarter
FS - 06:19 AGUAYO, R. 23 yd field goal, 12-77 5:28

Second Quarter
NEV - 11:31 WIMBERLY, Brandon 11 yd pass from COMBS, Devin (ZUZO, Brent kick), 4-28 2:02
FS - 03:21 SHAW, K. 24 yd pass from WINSTON, J. (AGUAYO, R. kick), 7-92 2:33
FS - 00:38 GREENE, R. 24 yd pass from WINSTON, J. (AGUAYO, R. kick), 4-56 1:12

Third Quarter
FS -14:29 FREEMAN, D. 6 yd run (AGUAYO, R. kick), 2-66 0:25
FS -12:47 WILLIAMS, K. 65 yd run (AGUAYO, R. kick), 1-65 0:08
FS - 10:06 WILDER, J. 1 yd run (AGUAYO, R. kick), 4-61 1:17
FS - 04:41 WINSTON, J. 10 yd run (AGUAYO, R. kick), 5-45 1:56
FS -00:58 AGUAYO, R. 33 yd field goal, 7-62 2:14

Fourth Quarter
07:11 FS - STEVENSON, F. 1 yd run (AGUAYO, R. kick), 9-69 4:42 7 - 55
02:48 FS - GREEN, R. 1 yd run (AGUAYO, R. kick), 6-64 2:45

	NEV	FSU
First downs	13	29
Rushes-yards	5	15
Passing	7	11
Comp-Att-Int	13-24-1	17-22-1
Return Yards	0	11.7
Punts-Avg.	45.9	53.0
Fumbles-Lost	0-0	0-0
Penalties-Yards	7-80	6-45
Time of Possession	33:01	26:59

DOAK CAMPBELL STADIUM | SEPTEMBER 21, 2013

FLORIDA STATE 54
BETHUNE-COOKMAN 6

OFF TO THE RACES
WINSTON THROWS FOR 148 YARDS

BY COREY CLARK

If No. 8 Florida State was taking FCS opponent Bethune-Cookman lightly on Saturday night, it certainly didn't show.

The Seminoles controlled the game from start to finish, scoring first on a Telvin Smith 68-yard interception return on the first drive of the game and then pouring it on from there in an eventual 54-6 win over the Wildcats at Doak Campbell Stadium.

"I'm very proud of our team," FSU head coach Jimbo Fisher said. "I thought we went in and did the things we had to do to win the game. Still a lot of room for improvement, in my opinion. I think we have to clean some things up.

"... We've got a lot of room to grow, but we did the things we had to do."

Florida State redshirt freshman quarterback Jameis Winston finished 10 of 19 for 148 yards and two touchdowns – including a spectacular 11-yard scoring strike to Kelvin Benjamin after the QB spun past one BCU defender in the pocket and then shook off another rusher before making the throw.

It seems as if every game Winston has at least one highlight-reel play. That was the

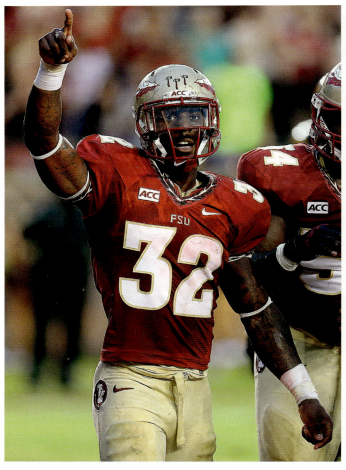

James Wilder Jr. celebrates his second quarter touchdown with fans. *Photo By: Mike Ewen/Democrat*

one on Saturday night. Even though afterward both the head coach and the quarterback said he made a mistake.

"It was supposed to be a hot (route)," Winston said. "But obviously God blessed me

Falling backward and escaping the grasp of Bethune-Cookman's Tavarus Dantzler, FSU quarterback Jameis Winston throws a touchdown pass that electrified the Seminole crowd. FSU used a stifling defense, a potent running game and enough Winston passes to roll over the Bethune-Cookman Wildcats, 33-0, in the first half. *Photo By: Mike Ewen/Democrat*

with the talent. I shook him off and then Kelvin was just right there. ... Kelvin made a great play.

"But that will be a negative in the film room."

It was a positive on the field, however, as he found Benjamin in the end zone for the first time this season.

"He can extend plays," Benjamin said. "I just kept running across the field and when I saw them miss that tackle he looked at me right dead in the eyes and threw it."

Junior running back Devonta Freeman had his second straight 100-yard rushing performance (10 carries for 112 yards and a score)

When the Seminoles get going, they don't slow down, as was the case when Terrence Brooks (No. 31) upended Bethune-Cookman's Anthony Jordan. *Photo By: Mike Ewen/Democrat*

and converted safety Karlos Williams continued his lightning-quick transformation with nine carries for 83 yards and two scores. All in the second half.

The Florida State offense rolled up 492 total yards against the overmatched Wildcats (3-1) and didn't punt until early in the fourth quarter. The Seminoles finished with 266 yards rushing on just 36 attempts (7.4 yards per carry).

"Everybody just does their job," junior offensive tackle Cameron Erving said. "That's what we harp on. That's what we tell each other. Just do your job. ... It's great to know we're having success on offense right now, but it's only three games. We've still got nine promised.

"So we just try to keep building what we have every game."

After giving up six first downs on the Wildcats' first two drives of the game, the Florida State first-team defense dominated the rest of the half, limiting the visitors to just 45 total yards on their next six drives.

Smith had the Seminoles' first defensive score of the season and sophomore linebacker Terrence Smith, filling in for the suspended Christian Jones, had eight of his game-high 12 tackles in the first half.

Not that any of the FSU defenders seemed all that pleased afterward. They did hold the Wildcats to just six points. But Bethune-Cookman was 9 of 18 on third downs and finished with 18 first downs – many coming in the second half when the game was already over.

"We've got to go back on Monday and get back to the fundamentals and get right," Telvin Smith said. "We're probably going to get yelled at for that one."

Winston isn't likely to get yelled at for his performance. Though he finished with more incompletions against Bethune (nine) than he had the first two games combined (five), he did have two touchdown passes dropped and another first-down pass slip through the hands of Freeman.

And for the second straight week he was perfect in the second half, completing all three of his passes for 36 yards and a touchdown to Rashad Greene, who dropped a would-be score in the first quarter.

"That kid has a strong arm," said Bethune-Cookman coach Brian Jenkins. "You are looking at a future Heisman Trophy winner. I don't know if there is a better quarterback in the country right now."

Not that Winston was striking any stiff-arm poses afterward. He was far from satisfied with his performance afterward.

When he was jokingly asked what was up with Greene dropping that pass, Winston immediately responded: "What's up with me overthrowing Nick O'Leary in the end zone? That (drop) is once in a lifetime. That's going to happen. That's football. It was raining out there.

"Everything was going our way today. Everything was going our way. I was making bad decisions out there. I was just making bad decisions. But the team did great."

More than anything the team did what it had to do. It took care of an outmanned, inferior opponent quickly.

The Seminoles had a 33-0 lead at halftime and buried an opponent that had just beaten an FBS school (albeit Florida International) by three touchdowns the previous week.

BOX SCORE

FLORIDA STATE 54, BETHUNE-COOKMAN 6

FSU	10	23	21	0 —	54
BC	0	0	6	0 —	6

First Quarter
FSU— Telvin Smith 68 INT return (Roberto Aguayo kick), 8:39.
FSU— Aguayo 45 FG, 2:33.

Second Quarter
FSU— Safety
FSU— Kelvin Benjamin 11 pass from Jameis Winston (Aguayo kick), 12:11.
FSU— James Wilder Jr. 2 run (Aguayo kick), 5:49.
FSU— Devonta Freeman 1 run (Aguayo kick), 1:13

Third Quarter
FSU— Rashad Greene 19 pass from Winston (Aguayo kick), 13:39.
BCU— Jackie Wilson 7 run (kick failed), 8:21.
FSU— Karlos Williams 3 run (Aguayo kick), 6:15.
FSU— Karlos Williams 1 run (Aguayo kick), 0:46.
A—74,841.

	FSU	BC
First downs	26	18
Rushes-yards	36-266	56-182
Passing	226	60
Comp-Att-Int	13-25-0	8-17-1
Return Yards	86	104
Punts-Avg.	0-0.0	1-6.0
Fumbles-Lost	1-1	2-0
Penalties-Yards	3-25	8-59
Time of Possession	24:01	35:59

FSU FEATURE

CHRISTIAN JONES & LAMARCUS JOYNER

BIG SEASON STARTED WITH BIG RETURNS

JONES, JOYNER PASSED ON NFL TO HELP FSU CHASE TITLE

BY IRA SCHOFFEL

Immediately after Florida State dismissed "BCS buster" Northern Illinois in the Orange Bowl on Jan. 1, 2013, Seminoles head coach Jimbo Fisher turned his attention to the future.

Not just recruiting incoming freshmen for the 2013 signing class, but attempting to bring back several draft-eligible players who were leaning toward bolting early for the NFL.

In the end, three of those players did move on — defensive end Bjoern Werner and cornerback Xavier Rhodes went on to be first-round draft picks, and offensive tackle Menelik Watson became a second-rounder — but Fisher was relatively at ease with their decisions. Werner and Rhodes were almost locks to go early in the draft, and Watson's family financial struggle was a major factor.

But Fisher did have success with the two remaining juniors from 2012, defensive back Lamarcus Joyner and linebacker Christian Jones, and their returns played a major role in kick-starting the Seminoles' run to the 2013 BCS national championship.

Christian Jones moves at the snap of the ball as the Florida State Seminoles battle the Florida Gators at Ben Hill Griffin Stadium in Gainesville on Nov. 30, 2013.
Photo By: Glenn Beil/Democrat

First came Joyner's statement on Jan. 3: "Coach Fisher and I aren't finished with what we started here," Joyner said. "He said from day one I was going to be one of those guys that was going to help turn this program around. We've started down the right path so far but we're still not finished. This wasn't a decision I could make just for myself but for my family in order to help them down the road, which is why I'm going to stay at Florida State for my last season."

Then came Jones' announcement on Jan. 14: "I've always talked with some of the guys I came in with and we've always talked about finishing together and that's also something I wanted to do. This is the best decision for me and my family. I'm looking forward to coming back, working hard, improving my game but also helping Florida State continue with the success we've had."

Those decisions were huge for the Seminoles for several reasons. First, the obvious: Jones was the top tackler (95 stops, seven for loss) on one of the nation's best defenses, and Joyner had just been named an All-ACC first-team safety.

Bringing back those pieces would provide a boost for any program, but particularly one that already was losing several seniors to the draft and would be introducing a new defensive coordinator during the offseason. It also sent a message to the Seminoles' returning players and incoming recruits that two of the team's leaders were fully committed to Fisher's vision for the program.

"It let me know that, 'OK, I've got some people backing me, with the same mindset that I have,'" senior linebacker Telvin Smith said. "They came in with me. And I remember we said something when we first stepped foot on campus: 'We're not leaving unless we're the best.' And that's what we've been playing for all four years.

"So when they said they were coming back, I knew we were on a roll."

Jones admits now that he originally was planning to go pro after his junior season. While he wasn't projected to be drafted until the second round, he figured his size — 6-foot-4, 235 pounds — and speed would impress NFL scouts in workouts.

But after talking to Fisher, hearing about new coordinator Jeremy Pruitt's schemes and considering all the talent the Seminoles had coming back, Jones decided to make one last push for a national championship.

"I knew when I decided to come back that we had a good group of guys coming back," Jones said. "So that kind of got me excited about this whole process. Right now, I'm just happy — loss of words. All this hard work that we put in during the offseason and the spring, it's all paying off.

"And we're finally where we want to be."

Lamarcus Joyner eyes the ball carrier as Florida State visits Heinz Field in Pittsburgh, Pa., for the opening night of the 2013 football season against the Pittsburgh Panthers.
Photo By: Glenn Beil/Democrat

ALUMNI STADIUM | SEPTEMBER 28, 2013

FLORIDA STATE 48
BOSTON COLLEGE 34

'NOLES SHRUG OFF EAGLES

FSU RALLIES FROM 14-POINT DEFICIT TO SCORE ROAD WIN

BY IRA SCHOFFEL

CHESTNUT HILL, Mass. — Boston College had so many of the ingredients in place for an upset here Saturday night.

The Eagles looked terrible in their previous game but had two weeks to prepare for No. 8 Florida State. They were playing at home against a team favored by 20-plus points on the road. And they sprinted out to an early two-touchdown lead, which should have put pressure on the Seminoles' redshirt freshman quarterback.

Unfortunately for the Eagles, Jameis Winston had another recipe in mind.

After completing just two of his first six passes, Winston went on a tear in the second quarter, completing seven consecutive throws — three for touchdowns — to put FSU back in command, and the Seminoles out-dueled Boston College down the stretch for a 48-34 victory.

"We knew this was going to be a very tough football game going in," said FSU Coach Jimbo Fisher, whose team improved to 4-0 and 2-0 in the ACC. "Boston College is always a very physical, tough football team. ... They caught us with some things and made some plays and got

Kelvin Benjamin makes a leaping catch as the 8th-ranked Florida State Seminoles take a lead into the half against the Boston College Eagles. *Photo By: Glenn Beil/Democrat*

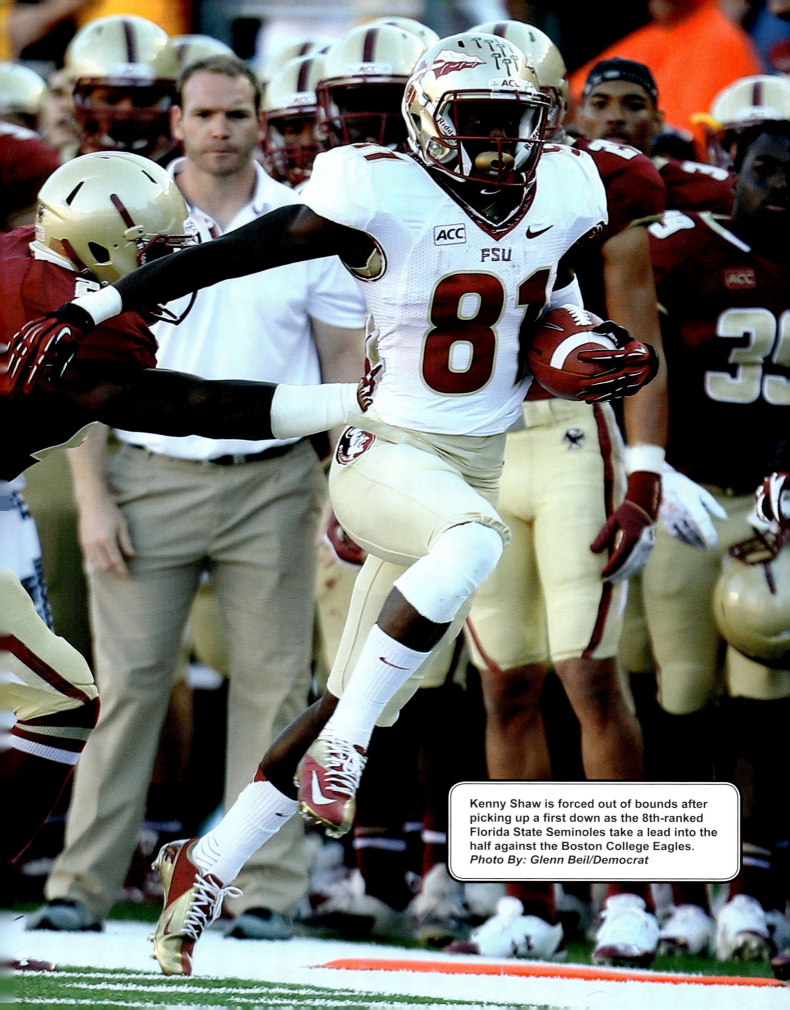

Kenny Shaw is forced out of bounds after picking up a first down as the 8th-ranked Florida State Seminoles take a lead into the half against the Boston College Eagles.
Photo By: Glenn Beil/Democrat

Above: Timmy Jernigan, 8, moves in to tackle BC quarterback Chase Rettig. *Photo By: Glenn Beil/Democrat*

Facing Page: Kelvin Benjamin drags BC defender C.J. Williams on his way to a first down as the 8th-ranked Florida State Seminoles take down the Boston College Eagles 48-34 at Alumni Stadium in Chestnut Hill, Mass. *Photo By: Glenn Beil/Democrat*

us behind early. But the kids kept a lot of poise in the game, I felt."

They needed every bit of it.

The Seminoles' defense, which has made a habit of getting off to slow starts early this season, struggled mightily against the Eagles' power running game and ensuing throwback passes.

BC running back Andre Williams plowed through the heart of the Seminoles' defensive front for 99 yards in the first half, and he finished with 149 for the game on 28 carries. And every time it seemed that FSU's defense might be in place to stop the run, Eagles quarterback Chase Rettig burned them with a misdirecton pass.

With a pair of short touchdown strikes and another drive that led to a field goal, Rettig gave the Eagles a 17-3 lead early in the second quarter.

Then Winston and company went to work.

First, he connected with junior wide receiver Rashad Greene on a 56-yard touchdown strike — the longest scoring throw of Winston's young career. Then he capped off an eight-play, 70-yard drive with a 10-yard TD toss to fullback Chad Abram to tie the game at 17-17.

And on his next possession, Winston one-upped his own incredible play from a week

earlier, when he shrugged off a pair of would-be tacklers in the backfield, spun out and delivered an off-balance touchdown pass. Against Bethune-Cookman, it resulted in an 11-yard touchdown pass to Kelvin Benjamin; on Saturday, it went for 55 yards and a score to Kenny Shaw.

"I was amazed," Benjamin said of Winston's dramatic play. "Shaking off the tackler and then getting it down to Kenny, and Kenny making that great catch. I was like, 'Man, that's crazy.' It was real exciting though."

"I just wanted to score a touchdown before the half, and Kenny made a great play," Winston said. "He's an outstanding talent, and he made an outstanding play."

The play was not simply astonishing, but it gave the Seminoles a 24-17 advantage and much-needed momentum entering halftime.

"That's the type of play we expect from him," said FSU linebacker Telvin Smith, who led the Seminoles with 10 tackles. "It was devastating giving up that big play before the half," said first-year Boston College coach Steve Addazio. "We had the kid on the ground."

Boston College (2-2, 1-1 ACC) was not done yet, however. While many in the Alumni Stadium crowd of 40,129 headed for the exits when the Seminoles surged ahead in the third quarter, 38-20, the Eagles would make things interesting once again.

Rettig, who had an uneven night (18-of-28 passing for 197 yards and two interceptions), connected on a pair of late touchdowns. First, he found running back Myles Willis streaking down the right sideline for a 52-yard score, and then he connected with C.J. Parsons on a 17-yard touchdown strike.

That was Parsons' second TD of the night, and the fourth for Rettig. But after a rocky effort, FSU's defense stepped up once more as freshman defensive back Nate Andrews picked off Rettig's final pass near the goal line to preserve the win.

"We have to learn to start better," Fisher said. "We had some critical mistakes. ... We did some things I've never seen us do before, but we overcame it."

Devonta Freeman looks for an opening as the 8th ranked Florida State Seminoles take a lead into the half against the Boston College Eagles.
Photo By: Glenn Beil/Democrat

BOX SCORE
FLORIDA STATE 48, BOSTON COLLEGE 34

FSU	3	21	14	10 —	48
Boston	14	3	10	7 —	34

First Quarter
BC- 09:58 C.J. Parsons 6 Yd Pass From Chase Rettig (Nate Freese Kick), 8-36 4:05
FS- 06:34 Roberto Aguayo 40 Yd field goal, 7-58 3:24
BC- 01:46 Jake Sinkovec 3 Yd Pass From Chase Rettig (Nate Freese Kick), 10-75 4:48

Second Quarter
BC- 11:19 Freese, N 24 yd field goal, 8-55 4:04
FS- 10:35 Rashad Greene. 56 yd PASS (AGUAYO, R. kick), 2-80 0:44
FS- 1:49 Chad Abraham. 10 yd PASS (AGUAYO, R. kock), 7-80 2:55
FS - :00 Kenny Shaw. 55 yd PASS (AGUAYO, R. kick), 7-80 2:55

Third Quarter
BC- 11:52 Nate Freese 24 Yd field goal, 6-19 3:08
FS- 09:06 Rashad Greene 10 Yd Pass From Jameis Winston (Roberto Aguayo Kick), 9-80 2:46
FS- 03:42 Karlos Williams 1 Yd Run (Roberto Aguayo Kick) Watch Highlight, 9-60 3:48
BC- 02:10 Myles Willis 52 Yd Pass From Chase Rettig (Nate Freese Kick), 5-79 1:32

Fourth Quarter
FS- 14:07 Roberto Aguayo 20 Yd field goal, 9-80 3:03
FS- 13:41 P.J. Williams 20 Yd Interception Return (Roberto Aguayo Kick)
BC- 09:44 C.J. Parsons 17 Yd Pass From Chase Rettig (Nate Freese Kick), 7-75 3:57

	FSU	Boston
First downs	25	22
Rushes-yards	184	210
Passing	12	10
Comp-Att-Int	17-27-1	18-28-2
Return Yards	72	231
Punts-Avg.	4-40	4-35
Fumbles-Lost	1-0	0-0
Penalties-Yards	5-44	3-44
Time of Possession	26:44	33:16

DOAK CAMPBELL STADIUM | OCTOBER 5, 2013

FLORIDA STATE 63
MARYLAND 0

WINSTON, 'NOLES STOMP MARYLAND, 63-0

BY COREY CLARK

It was billed as an "ACC Showdown" between two undefeated teams ranked in the Top 25.

But only one of them actually showed up.

The No. 8 Florida State Seminoles got another jaw-dropping performance from their quarterback and a dominant outing from their defense in a 63-0 beatdown of No. 25 Maryland on Saturday at Doak Campbell Stadium.

The 63-point margin of victory tied for the largest ever suffered by a nationally ranked team (No. 11 Texas lost to UCLA, 66-3, in 1997).

"We got going on offense and played very well, but I thought the defense was the story of the day," FSU head Coach Jimbo Fisher said. "I thought they really took the show. I thought they dominated from the start to the finish."

A week after allowing 34 points to a struggling Boston College offense, the Florida State defense allowed exactly 34 less than that on Saturday, giving first-year defensive coordinator Jeremy Pruitt the first shutout of his career.

"To finally get that goose egg, that's big time," senior linebacker Telvin Smith said. "All week in practice, we were a lot more focused and a lot more detailed. Just because of Boston College. Everybody was on the same page, every-

FSU's Jameis Winston fires a strike to receiver Kenny Shaw against Maryland. *Photo By: Mike Ewen/Democrat*

body had the same mindset — come out, start fast and dominate throughout the whole game."

And on the other side of the ball, well, Jameis Winston was once again Jameis Winston.

The redshirt freshman QB was 23 of 32 for 393 yards and five touchdowns, including yet another highlight-reel play in which he somehow avoided a sack in the pocket, ran to

Nick O'Leary, left, and L.A. Goree go head to head as Florida State hosts the 25th-ranked Maryland Terrapins on Oct. 5, 2013. Photo By: Glenn Beil/Democrat

his right and found tight end Nick O'Leary in the end zone for a 12-yard touchdown.

"I was having flashbacks, just seeing him do that all the time," said junior receiver Rashad Greene, who finished with four catches for 108 yards. "And the only thing I could do was laugh. And no disrespect to anybody. I saw Jimbo doing the same thing. It's amazing how a guy can do things like that and still make plays."

Led by Winston's magnificent performance, all the Florida State offense did was score touchdowns on eight consecutive drives, with the star quarterback finishing off five of them with touchdown passes.

Not only did the Terrapins (4-1, 0-1) get trounced, rushing for just 33 yards on 25 carries, but starting quarterback C.J. Brown was lost for the game with a concussion in the second quarter.

"If you can't run the ball, that makes it tough," Maryland head Coach Randy Edsall said. "That was one of the match-ups I was concerned about coming into the game. You know, our offensive line against them.

"They made us one-dimensional. Give them credit. It makes it very, very difficult."

Meanwhile, after their relatively slow start, the Seminoles absolutely torched a Maryland defense that had allowed just four touchdowns all season coming into Saturday.

"We put up 63 points," said senior receiver Kenny Shaw, who had five catches for 96 yards and a touchdown. "What more can you ask for?"

It was an ugly farewell for Maryland, which is playing its final season in the ACC before bolting for the Big Ten.

Florida State, which is now 5-0 overall and 3-0 in the conference, has next week off before it takes on No. 3 Clemson in Death Valley.

WELCOME TO WINSTON'S WACKY WORLD

BY IRA SCHOFFEL

While waiting for postgame interviews to begin Saturday afternoon, a veteran journalist walked up to a longtime Florida State staff member and asked a question.

"Is he better than EJ?" the reporter asked.

"EJ?" the staffer deadpanned. "He might be better than M.J."

That is the level of absurdity we have reached here, people.

The reporter's question — whether Jameis Winston is a better quarterback than first-round pick and NFL starter EJ Manuel — was asked facetiously. As in, of course he is.

And the staff member's response was funny, of course, because it made reference to arguably the greatest athlete and competitor of our generation: Michael Jordan.

Crazy talk, right?

Absolutely it is.

When a redshirt freshman has played all of five college football games, you don't joke mockingly about how much better he is than a guy who has won games in the NFL. And you certainly don't compare him to a freaking living legend.

But this is what this kid has done to us. He's reserving us all seats on the crazy train.

Jameis Winston is not rewriting the rules; he's tearing them up and saying they don't exist.

Quarterbacks don't play this well this early. They don't make all of these throws and display this type of poise at the age of 19. They certainly don't routinely break free from the grasp of defensive linemen and linebackers, spin away from pressure and calmly throw touchdown passes.

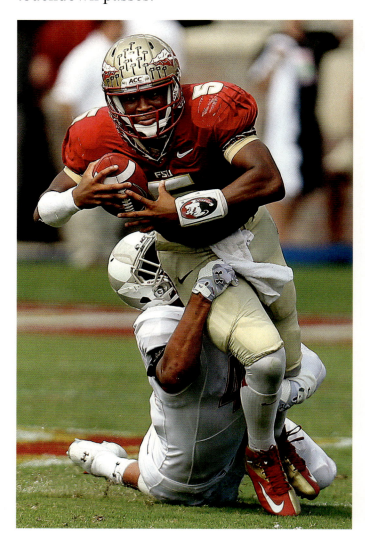

FSU quarterback Jameis Winston drags a Terrapin defender for a couple of extra yards. FSU's defensive unit came to play, delivering a shutout against the Maryland Terrapins, 63-0.
Photo By: Mike Ewen/Democrat

Terrence Brooks breaks up a pass attempt as Florida State pounds the 25th-ranked Maryland Terrapins on Oct. 5, 2013 at Doak Campbell Stadium. *Photo By: Glenn Beil/Democrat*

For most college quarterbacks, that type of play might happen once in a career.

This guy does it every week.

At Boston College, it was so he could throw a bomb to Kenny Shaw. One week earlier, it was to connect with Kelvin Benjamin on a score. On Saturday, it was to hit tight end Nick O'Leary for the fourth of five touchdown passes.

"Being tackled wasn't even on my mind," Winston said of his latest crazy play, when he tossed aside Maryland linebacker Yannik Cudjoe-Virgil. "I think it was third down. And I just knew. I was like, 'Golly. I've got to get out of this.' And Nick was wide open."

Golly, indeed.

"It's just something you can't even coach," senior wide receiver Kenny Shaw said of Winston's ability to shrug off tacklers and still make accurate throws on the run. "You can't coach that in a quarterback."

Apparently, this is going to be his thing, though.

My wife likes to crochet. I enjoy rac-

quetball. Jameis Winston shrugs off 250-pound defenders and throws for touchdowns.

If this is going to be his signature move, we need to give it a name already. The Winston whirl? The Jameis juke?

By the time Florida State's 63-0 shellacking of No. 25 Maryland was complete Saturday, the Seminoles had amassed 614 yards of total offense. Winston accounted for 417 of them — 393 passing and 24 rushing — and he now has thrown for 17 touchdowns with two interceptions.

Crazy. Crazy. Crazy.

I'm not even sure Florida State Coach Jimbo Fisher knows what to make of it.

Did you catch Fisher's expression after the latest Winston whirl? His smile was priceless. A) Because of what it said; and B) Because it proved Fisher actually is capable of smiling during a game.

See what I mean about Winston scrapping the rules?

When Fisher was asked about the smile in his postgame press conference, he explained what we already knew: "I was mad 'cause he should have done some something else."

Yeah, we know, Coach.

The room erupted in laughter. Not because Fisher was kidding, but because of the absurdity of it all.

Yes, Winston might have done something wrong on the play. He probably could have dumped the ball off to tailback James Wilder Jr. in the flat before Cudjoe-Virgil was able to get past left tackle Cameron Erving.

Perhaps, as Fisher told Winston when he returned to the sideline, he held the ball too long.

But the great ones don't follow the sheet music. They improvise.

"When he has that smirk, he's about to tell me that I did something wrong," Winston said. "But he's also about to tell me, 'Hey, great play. But don't let it happen again.'"

Oh, I don't think Fisher will be saying that any time soon.

'Cause that would really be crazy.

Nick O'Leary makes a leaping touchdown catch on Oct. 5, 2013 at Doak Campbell Stadium.
Photo By: Glenn Beil/Democrat

BOX SCORE

FLORIDA STATE 63, MARYLAND 0

Maryland	0	0	0	0	— 0
Florida State	7	14	21	21	— 63

First Quarter
FS- 8:14 K. Williams 1 yd Run (R. Aguayo kick), 10-77 4:40

Second Quarter
FS- 06:15 D. Freeman 5 yd run (Aguayo kick), 9-80 4:11
FS- 00:28 K. Benjamin 5 yd pass from J. Winston (R. Aguayo kick), 9-78 3:20

Third Quarter
FS- 12:18 N. O'Leary 8 yd pass from J. Winston (R. Aguayo kick), 7-94 2:38
FS- 09:47 K. Shaw 21 yd pass from J. Winston (R. Aguayo kick), 6-55 1:43
FS- 1:50 N. O'Leary 12 yd pass from J. Winston (R. Aguayo kick) 10-83 5:15

Fourth Quarter
FS- 14:56 K. Benjamin 21 yd pass from J. Winston (R. Aguayo kick), 1-21 0:04
FS- 11:28 K. Williams 17 yd Run (R. Aguayo kick), 7-66 2:03
FS- 09:49 J. Coker 24 yd run (R. Aguayo kick), 1-24 0:07

	UMD	FSU
First downs	9	33
Rushes-yards	1-33	12-183
Passing	8	21
Comp-Att-Int	15-32-0	26-39-0
Return Yards	73	62
Punts-Avg.	11-38.2	4-42
Fumbles-Lost	3-1	1-0
Penalties-Yards	4-40	4-26
Time of Possession	25:45	34:15

MEMORIAL STADIUM | OCTOBER 19, 2013

FLORIDA STATE   51
CLEMSON   14

HISTORIC TRIP
FSU FIRST TEAM TO SCORE 50 POINTS AT CLEMSON

BY COREY CLARK

CLEMSON, S.C. — Heading into Saturday night's highly anticipated, much-hyped Top-5 showdown, the Florida State Seminoles heard all week how they hadn't won a game in Death Valley since 2001.

Well, they have now.

Thanks to a superstar freshman quarterback, an array of playmaking receivers and a dominant defense, the No. 5 Seminoles ended the streak in emphatic fashion with a 51-14 win over the No. 3 Tigers in front of 83,428 at Memorial Stadium.

With the win, Florida State (6-0 overall and 4-0 in the ACC) took a stranglehold on the Atlantic Division race and kept itself very much in the national championship conversation.

The Seminoles are also the first team to score 50 points against Clemson at Death Valley.

"I wasn't surprised, we worked and prepared for this game for two weeks," FSU receiver Rashad Greene said. "We came here expecting to win."

And in the battle of Heisman hopeful quarterbacks, it was Florida State quarterback Jameis Winston who had an enormous night. The redshirt freshman was 22 of 34 for 444

Jameis Winston celebrates a touchdown throw as the Florida State Seminoles visit the Clemson Tigers at Memorial Stadium. *Photo By: Glenn Beil/Democrat.*

Rashad Greene sheds a defender after making a catch along the sidelines at Memorial Stadium in Clemson, S.C.
Photo By: Glenn Beil/Democrat

Kelvin Benjamin makes a leaping touchdown catch as the 5th-ranked Florida State Seminoles visit the 3rd-ranked Clemson Tigers.
Photo By: Glenn Beil/Democrat

yards and three touchdowns for the Seminoles, while Clemson's fifth-year senior Tajh Boyd was 17 of 37 for 156 yards and three total turnovers.

"I could tell in the locker room how things were going to happen tonight," Winston said. "Clemson is an amazing team, but I knew we were going to play our best. And when we play our best, we are hard to beat."

Greene and tight end Nick O'Leary were the beneficiaries of Winston's hot hand, combining on 13 receptions for 307 yards. Greene also had two touchdown receptions.

On the first play of the game, FSU's Lamarcus Joyner stripped the ball from Clemson tight end Stanton Seckinger and fellow senior Terrence Brooks recovered at the Clemson 34.

Three plays later Winston lofted a pass toward the goal line to sophomore receiver Kelvin Benjamin, who leapt high over a Clemson defender and snared the ball for a 22-yard touchdown.

After the FSU defense held on the next series, the offense went right back to work. Starting at their own 12, the Seminoles drove 77 yards in 16 plays to get deep inside Tiger territory. But James Wilder Jr. was stuffed on third-and-two and FSU settled for a 28-yard field goal by Roberto Aguayo and a 10-0 lead.

"I am glad we started fast, that's what I really wanted," Brooks said. "It was nice to shut them up real quick."

But just when the Clemson fans thought the start couldn't get any worse, it did.

With a first down just inside FSU territory, Joyner came free on a blitz and blindsided Boyd, causing a fumble that was scooped up by Mario Edwards Jr. The sophomore defensive end sprinted 37 yards for a touchdown

Kenny Shaw celebrates with fans as the 5th-ranked Florida State Seminoles roll over the 3rd-ranked Clemson Tigers 51-14 at Memorial Stadium in Clemson, S.C. *Photo By: Glenn Beil/Democrat*

to give a stunning 17-0 FSU lead.

Clemson answered back with a 65-yard drive on its next possession, converting two big third downs along the way, and scored on a Sammy Watkins' two-yard TD catch with 51 seconds left in the first quarter.

After a rare ugly stretch by the FSU offense – a Winston interception was followed on the next drive by a false start, incompletion, timeout (to avoid delay of game penalty), rush for no gain and then another delay of game penalty – the freshman QB got right back to work on the next series.

Taking over at his own 5 after another stand by the FSU defense, Winston hit two short passes to give the Seminoles some breath-

ing room and then found Rashad Greene over the middle at the FSU 40.

The junior wideout made two Clemson defenders missed and then sprinted untouched to the end zone for a 72-yard score. The Seminoles were up 24-7 with still half the second quarter left to play.

Joyner then accounted for his third turnover of the half on Clemson's next possession, intercepting a Boyd pass and returning it to the FSU 23.

Winston then led a time-consuming field goal drive, which included picking up a second-and-30 on back-to-back throws to Kenny Shaw. Aguayo's second field goal of the half, with two seconds left, gave the Seminoles a 27-7 lead at the break.

Winston finished the first half 14 of 22 for 242 yards, two touchdowns and the one interception. Florida State piled up 312 yards on 42 plays, while Clemson managed just 141 yards on 39 plays against the Seminoles' defense.

Boyd was just 11 of 24 in the first half for 99 yards. And the Clemson running backs had just seven carries for 26 yards.

The second half didn't start any better for the Tigers. After Florida State freshman Levonte "Kermit" Whitfield returned the opening kickoff 43 yards – and Clemson was tagged with a facemask on the play – the Seminoles drove 42 yards for another score.

Greene hauled in a tunnel screen on third down, split two defenders, spun past another and scored an 18-yard touchdown to all but put the game away.

Mario Edwards Jr. returns a fumble for a touchdown as the 5th-ranked Florida State Seminoles visit the 3rd-ranked Clemson Tigers at Memorial Stadium in Clemson, S.C.
Photo By: Glenn Beil/Democrat

BOX SCORE

FLORIDA STATE 51, CLEMSON 14

FSU	17	10	14	10 —	51
Clemson	7	0	0	7 —	14

First Quarter
FSU- 13:38 Jameis Winston pass complete to Kelvin Benjamin for 22 yards for TD. (Roberto Aguayo kick)
FSU- 4:18 Roberto Aguayo 28 yard field goal.
FSU- 3:07 Tajh Boyd sacked by Lamarcus Joyner, fumbled, forced by Lamarcus Joyner, recovered by FlaSt Mario Edwards Jr. at the Clem 37, Mario Edwards Jr. for 37 yards, to the Clem 0 for TD. Roberto (Aguayo kick).
C- 0:51 Tajh Boyd pass complete to Sammy Watkins 3 yards for TD. (Chandler Catanzaro kick).

Second Quarter
FSU- 7:08 Jameis Winston pass complete to Rashad Greene for 72 yards for a TD. (Roberto Aguayo kick)
FSU- 0:03 Roberto Aguayo 24 yard field goal.

Third Quarter
FSU- 13:33 Jameis Winston pass complete to Rashad Greene for 17 yards for a TD. (Roberto Aguayo kick).
FSU- 4:04 Jameis Winston rush for 4 yards for a TD. (Roberto Aguayo kick).

Fourth Quarter
FSU- 12:17 Devonta Freeman rush for 2 yards for a TD (Roberto Aguayo kick).
FSU- 4:41 Roberto Aguayo 20 yard field goal.
C- 0:13 Cole Stoudt rush for 2 yards for a TD. (Chandler Catanzaro kick).

	FSU	Clemson
First downs	30	26
Rushes-yards	122-566	123-326
Passing	444	203
Comp-Att-Int	22-35-1	22-45-2
Fumbles-Lost	0	2
Penalties-Yards	12-104	7-96
Time of Possession	35:13	24:39

FSU FEATURE

TELVIN SMITH

PLAYING WITH PURPOSE

LB SMITH DRAWS INSPIRATION FROM DEATH OF FATHER, BIRTH OF SON

BY COREY CLARK

It's not just that he never got to say goodbye that made it so painful. It's that, in the end, he rarely even said hello.

When the phone call came from his sister that afternoon, Telvin Smith was sitting in his room at Burt Reynolds Hall. It was a Sunday. In December. He was alone.

There are no words that can accurately describe the feeling that comes next, what that moment is like, when you hear that your father has died from a massive heart attack. At the age of 46.

The pain is so swift, so sudden, that it can literally drop you to your knees.

But for Telvin Smith, who was then a freshman linebacker on the Florida State football team, the anguish he felt was laced with anger. At himself.

"He never got to see me play a college game," Smith said of his father, Willie James Smith. "That's because I didn't want him to. I don't really know how to even explain it. I was going through some crazy stuff coming out of high school. It wasn't even anger (at my dad);

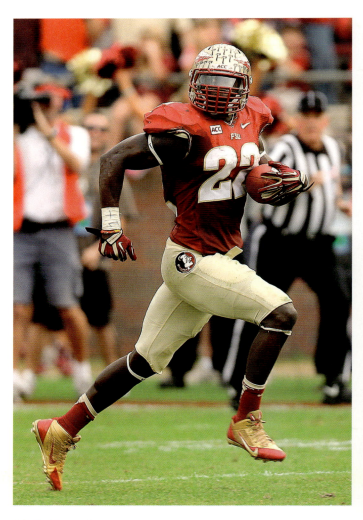

FSU's Telvin Smith races 79 yards for a touchdown on a first-quarter interception in an 80-14 win over Idaho.
Photo By: Mike Ewen/Democrat

Telvin Smith holds his son Triston Smith during FSU's Senior Day. The Florida State Seminoles used some big plays on the defense and a steady offensive attack to win 80-14 over Idaho. *Photo By: Mike Ewen/Democrat*

FSU's Telvin Smith races to recover a fumble by Wolfpack receiver Johnathan Alston. The Florida State Seminoles used a swarming defense to cause turnovers and Jameis Winston led the offense on the field as FSU took a 42-0 lead over the visiting North Carolina State Wolfpack. *Photo By: Mike Ewen/Democrat*

I don't know why, but I just let the relationship dwindle while I was here.

"And that hurts me so bad even to this day."

There are varying degrees of every emotion. But a deep regret might be the one that hurts most. It lingers the longest and can be the toughest to overcome.

For Smith, now a senior leading the No. 1 Seminoles in tackles, he says he's never really gotten past those final months of his father's life. When, for reasons he's still not ready to — or perhaps able to — explain, he would mostly ignore his phone calls.

"There were so many times he'd push," Smith said. "And weeks before he died, he was trying to contact me, trying to call me. But I just wasn't picking up.

"And I just felt like I let myself down because I didn't push to have that relationship."

Smith never lived with his father, who like him was born and raised in Valdosta, Ga. But throughout his childhood and high school days, he says he did have a close relationship with him. Willie, who was known as "Tony Tooley" by virtually everyone he ever met, was there at all of Telvin's games for Lowndes High School.

The son remembers after one game in particular, a 10-7 loss to Northside Warner-Robins during his senior year, when he sobbed in his father's arms until he was out of tears.

"He was there holding me up," Smith said. "He was just the rock that held me together as a player."

Just like that, on Dec. 19, 2010, the rock was gone.

And then, so was Smith.

He left his room that day and just got into his car. He wasn't driving anywhere in particular, just away from where he had been.

Word began to spread among his teammates, though. And it wasn't long until he got a call from then-position Coach Greg Hudson.

"You better get your butt to the house right now," Hudson told him. "Come on, man. Get over here."

Reluctantly, Smith agreed.

When he arrived, he was met by virtually the entire FSU linebacker corps. There were hugs. Tears. Kind words. More hugs. More tears.

As much as he appreciated the gesture, it didn't really help.

"I felt no comfort from anyone at that time because I knew the mistake I had made by not talking to him," Smith said. "I would never be able to talk to him again. And really that's all I wanted, for him to be standing in front of me or sitting beside me."

Telvin Smith is one of the most emotional players Jimbo Fisher has ever coached. At just 218 pounds, he's built more like a safety than a linebacker, yet Smith continually wreaks havoc on opposing offenses.

"He's really matured," Fisher said. "He's become a leader for this football team."

And he always seems to play inspired. With good reason, it turns out.

The first game after Willie James Smith's death was the 2010 Chick-fil-A Bowl in Atlanta. Telvin dedicated the game to his father. And even though he didn't play a down on defense that night, he still had three tackles because he was a terror on special teams.

"I tried to make every tackle," Smith said.

And he has been trying to do so ever since. Not just for him. Not just for his teammates. And not just for his father.

Smith now has a 2-year-old son named Triston, who lives in his hometown of Valdosta. The toddler comes to every game at Doak Campbell Stadium and when Smith goes back home, he tries to take Triston to as many Lowndes High games as possible.

"I'm not going to force football on him or anything," he said. "But he loves it so far. He says he wants to be like his daddy. He knows I'm No. 22. And he already knows the Florida State chant."

What Smith doesn't want his son to ever know is that pain. That regret.

He says there's not a day that goes by that he doesn't think about his father. Though Willie never played football, he seemed to take incredible joy in watching his son on Friday nights. He'd travel all over the state to do so.

That big personality that Telvin has? That bigger smile? They both come from Willie, Smith says.

He then shakes his head, as his eyes to begin to water.

"When I lost him, to this day, I still don't kind of comprehend it," Smith said. "I wish so many times that he was here. Not a day goes by that I don't think about it, wishing I could talk to him more, wishing I could make it right."

He pauses. Just for a moment.

Then his eyes brighten. And that Telvin Smith smile begins to appear.

"The way I started to see it, though, is God took my father but He gave me a son," Smith said. "And He said, 'Now, here's your chance. Show him what you didn't have and give him everything he needs. Don't let him make the same mistakes you did. Just be there for him.'

"And that's what I'm going to do."

DOAK CAMPBELL STADIUM | OCTOBER 26, 2013

FLORIDA STATE 49
NC STATE 17

WHAT LETDOWN? FSU TROUNCES N.C. STATE

NO. 3 SEMINOLES EXPLODE TO HUGE LEAD, ROLL PAST WOLFPACK, 49-17

BY COREY CLARK

They were coming off their biggest win in more than a decade and knew they had a Top-10 showdown with rival Miami next weekend.

So it would have been natural, maybe even expected, for the No. 3 Florida State football team to have a letdown on Saturday against unranked North Carolina State.

Yeah, not quite. The Seminoles were up 35-0 less than 13 minutes into the game and cruised to a 49-17 victory over the Wolfpack.

"We had to make a statement that last week was not a fluke," FSU quarterback Jameis Winston said of the 51-14 win over then-No. 3 Clemson. "And we had to show N.C. State team, that had a lot of confidence coming in this game ... we had to show them who the better team was today."

The Wolfpack, and everyone watching, realized that real quick.

"We hold ourselves to a high standard," junior receiver Rashad Greene said.

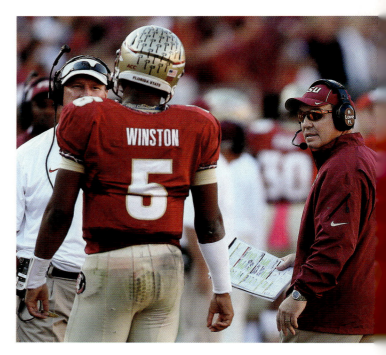

Head coach Jimbo Fisher talks to quarterback Jameis Winston after a touchdowh. Jimbo Fisher shut down the offense in the second half and FSU won 49-17.
Photo By: Mike Ewen/Democrat

"Nothing less. We know it's going to take every week, every practice, every game. And once a game is over, you have to sweep it under the rug. And that's what we're good at doing."

FSU fans had reason to cheer loudly and often in the first half as the Seminoles scored early against the Wolfpack. The Florida State Seminoles used a swarming defense to cause turnovers and Jameis Winston led the offense on the field as FSU took a 42-0 lead over the visiting North Carolina State Wolfpack. *Photo By: Mike Ewen/Democrat*

The Wolfpack got swept off a cliff in the first half on Saturday.

The game was so out of hand that Florida State didn't play its defensive starters for a single play in the second half. And the first-team offense took just six snaps.

FSU Coach Jimbo Fisher was far from happy with his second team on Saturday, but with the undefeated Hurricanes on the horizon, he didn't want to take any risks in a game that was already decided.

"You've got to be careful about injuries," said Fisher, whose team improved to 7-0 overall and 5-0 in the ACC. "And you've got to develop your young players. You've got to get those guys game time and get them on the field."

Winston finished 16 of 26 for 292 yards, three touchdowns and one interception in the victory. And Greene had eight catches for 137 yards and a touchdown. Greene's score was the final one of a stun-

Karlos Williams races for a first down on a fake punt in the second half as Marchez Coates defends.
Photo By: Mike Ewen/Democrat

ning first-quarter barrage that saw the Seminoles put up 35 points and 274 total yards.

He said it was a perfect pass from Winston.

"He threw me open," said Greene, who went over the 100-yard mark for the fourth time this season. "It was a post and he was able to throw me open. He made a great throw, and I was able to go run up under it."

As good as the offense was in the first half — and it was '90s good, again — the defense might have been better. The Florida State first-team held N.C. State to just five first downs.

Wolfpack starting quarterback Brandon Mitchell, who hadn't played since the first week of the season, was 5 of 16 with two interceptions against the Seminoles in the first half.

"Pretty much he chose the wrong defense to come start against," FSU senior defensive back Lamarcus Joyner said. "My hat's off to that guy, though. He came in and competed. He made no excuses. Played the whole entire game."

N.C. State's first six drives went like this: Interception, punt, punt, fumble, punt, interception.

Meanwhile, FSU's first five drives on Saturday went touchdown, touchdown, touchdown, touchdown, touchdown.

At the end of the first half, Florida State had 371 total yards. N.C. State had 85.

"It was crazy because it seemed like as fast as we got them off the field, we had to go right back on," junior defensive tackle Timmy Jernigan said. "Sometimes I was like, 'Dang, Jameis. Man, just incomplete one pass.' But it was just fun. It's fun when the offense is scoring like that and when the defense is playing at a high level."

Maybe there will be a "trap game" later on this season for the Seminoles. It certainly wasn't on Saturday, though.

"It felt awesome," Jones said. "Coach was stressing all week to not look at is a revenge game, but we knew how much this game meant to us. Those guys kind of put a halt to our season last year, so it felt good.

"Because they took something away from us last year."

This year, they just took a 49-17 thumping and headed back to Raleigh, N.C.

"It definitely felt good," senior safety Terrence Brooks said. "I was very hurt last year by that game and I'm pretty sure the whole 'Nole Nation was, too. But we were definitely not going to let that happen again."

BOX SCORE

FLORIDA STATE 49, N.C. STATE 17

N.C. State	0	0	10	7 —	17
FSU	35	7	0	7 —	49

First Quarter
FSU - Karlos Williams 18 run (Robert Aguayo kick), 13:02. Drive: 4-65, 1:25
FSU - Kelvin Benjamin 39 pass from Jameis Winston (Robert Aguayo kick), 11:12. Drive: 1-39, 0:08
FSU - Devonta Freeman 11 run (Robert Aguayo kick), 7:02. Drive: 7-62, 2:29.
FSU - Nick O'Leary 14 pass from Jameis Winston (Robert Aguayo kick), 6:09. Drive: 2-14, 0:11.
FSU - Rashad Greene 42 pass from Jameis Winston (Robert Aguayo kick), 2:02. Drive: 5-89, 1:55.

Second Quarter
FSU - Devonta Freeman 4 run (Robert Aguayo kick), 3:06. Drive: 6-54, 1:14.

Third Quarter
NCST - Niklas Sade 36 FG, 7:51. Drive: 12-75, 5:09.
NCST - Shardrach Thornton 72 run (Nicklas Sade kick), 0:59. Drive: 3-88, 0:57.

Fourth Quarter
NCST - Shardrach Thornton 1 run (Nicklas Sade kick), 7:16. Drive: 11-62, 3:50.
FSU - Kermit Whitfield 31 run (Robert Aguayo kick), 2:19. Drive: 9-79, 4:51.
Att. 80,389.

	N.C. State	FSU
First downs	16	30
Rushes-yards	42-188	34-224
Passing	128	342
Comp-Att-Int	17-33-2	20-34-2
Return Yards	44	79
Punts-Avg.	8-46.8	4-36.8
Fumbles-Lost	1-1	0-0
Penalties-Yards	2-13	3-30
Time of Possession	30:53	29:07

APPRECIATIVE BOWDEN LOOKS TOWARD THE FUTURE WITH FSU

LEGENDARY COACH MOVED BY OUTPOURING OF LOVE

BY JIM HENRY

Bobby Bowden wanted to enjoy the festivities.

Yet, the former Florida State coach, in a moment of candid reflection, admitted he couldn't have asked for more in his life and coaching career.

"I feel like I am the luckiest, I feel like I am (as) lucky as any guy who ever lived," Bowden said prior to being honored at the FSU-North Carolina State game at Doak Campbell Stadium.

"God has been good to me. Fifty-seven years of coaching, I survived it. And right now I feel good. When you get old, if your health is good, it don't make no difference. I've been very fortunate for my health."

More than an hour after meeting with the press, the Hall of Fame coach received a thunderous ovation from the crowd as he and his wife, Ann, emerged from the tunnel that leads onto the field.

More than 350 former players stood on both sides of the field to honor their coach and his first appearance at an FSU football game since his forced retirement following the 2009 season.

Bowden spoke to the crowd for a few minutes and planted Osceola's spear at midfield as fans stood and cheered.

Bobby Bowden was greeted by a thunderous ovation as he came on the field to plant the flaming spear during pre-game ceremonies at FSU on Oct. 26, 2013.
Photo By: Mike Ewen/Democrat

Bowden watched most of FSU's 49-17 victory over the Wolfpack from the president's box; when he wasn't granting interview requests from radio and television.

Bowden, who turned 84 in November, is also looking forward to working with Seminole Boosters, Inc., starting this year.

He signed a two-year deal with the organization to help raise money for Seminole athletics.

Bowden will make public and private appearances. The deal will pay him $250,000 annually with an option for a third year.

"When I quit coaching here, the thing I missed the most was not football. It was the Booster dinners," Bowden said.

"I did Booster dinners for 34 years. Every year I go to Tampa. Every year I go to Orlando. Every year I go to Miami. Twenty-five to 35 a year. You get pretty close to people, you get to know them pretty good. You know somebody for 34 years, play golf with them. I miss that, I miss that."

Bowden's return to FSU has been a festive affair.

He attended a sold-out golf tournament in his honor before the N.C. State game, and around 5,500 people paid to attend another event at the Civic Center.

Bowden admitted his emotions nearly got the best of him after seeing so many familiar faces and former players.

"It means a lot because I saw a lot of kids I haven't seen in years," Bowden said.

"It makes you feel good. It's funny folks, coaching 57 years like I did. I get a letter occasionally from a boy I coached 40 years ago, 50 years ago, 30 years ago. None of them mention football.

"None of them say, 'Boy, remember when I did this? Or remember when you did this?' They don't mention it. They tell me about their families, they tell me about their children and they tell me how much they appreciate what they learned at Florida State."

Bowden also admitted to a slight case of nerves about planting Osceola's spear at midfield prior to the game. Bowden planted

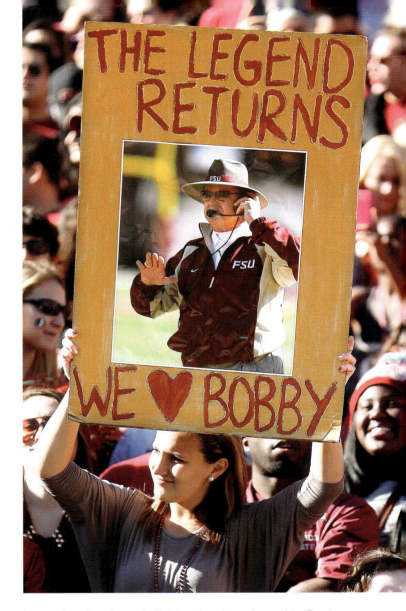

Legendary head coach Bobby Bowden returned to Doak Campbell Stadium and fans returned the love.
Photo By: Mike Ewen/Democrat

the spear in his final game in 2009 at the Gator Bowl in Jacksonville.

He was perfect this time, too.

"That's going to get me a little bit, that bothers me," Bowden said.

"It don't count, baby, unless that (spear) sticks. I was afraid I couldn't stick that thing in the ground at the Gator Bowl. I have to sweat that out today.

"I might have to take a mulligan."

DOAK CAMPBELL STADIUM | NOVEMBER 2, 2013

FLORIDA STATE 41
MIAMI 14

'NOLES IN A RUNAWAY

FSU EXPLODES FOR 20 POINTS IN SECOND HALF

BY COREY CLARK

For a half it felt like old times.

For a half it felt like one of those classic Florida State-Miami battles of yesteryear.

Then came the final two quarters.

The No. 3 Seminoles pummeled the No. 6 Hurricanes in the second half on Saturday night, outscoring them 20-0, en route to an emphatic 41-14 win in front of a Doak Campbell Stadium record crowd of 84,409.

"It was tough," FSU senior cornerback Lamarcus Joyner said. "Those guys are great football players. It was emotional, hard-nosed football. We needed that test."

And they passed it with flying colors.

Even with quarterback Jameis Winston having an "off night" by his remarkable standards, the Seminoles still beat the No. 6 team in the country by 27 points.

"It shows we're a great team," FSU head Coach Jimbo Fisher said. "It shows we're a complete team. ... This is a very good football team. And that's a very good football team. Beating them by four touchdowns? That doesn't happen very often."

Florida State improved to 8-0 on the season with the win and 6-0 in the ACC. A win next week at Wake Forest would wrap up the Atlantic Division title for the Seminoles. Meanwhile the Hurricanes play at Virginia Tech in an important Coastal Division battle.

"I give Florida State a lot of credit," Miami head coach Al Golden said. "That's an excellent team and a deep team. We have to

Above: Timmy Jernigan pumps up the crowd as Florida State hosts ACC and in-state rival the Miami Hurricanes in a match-up of Top-10 teams. *Photo By: Glenn Beil/Democrat*

Right: Telvin Smith celebrates after Florida State pounds ACC, and in-state rival, the Miami Hurricanes 41-14 in Tallahassee. *Photo By: Glenn Beil/Democrat*

FSU quarterback Jameis Winston raced for a first down before being brought down by Miami's Denzel Perryman in the first half.
Photo By: Mike Ewen/Democrat

play so much better than that and we did not."

After allowing 14 points and 175 yards in the first half, the Florida State defense shut down the Hurricanes in the final two quarters, limiting Miami to just 105 yards the rest of the way.

"It felt great," said cornerback P.J. Williams, who had a third-quarter interception. "We just had to come out and fight (in the second half) and give our offense some momentum."

Devonta Freeman scores a second touchdown as Florida State pounds ACC, and in-state rival, the Miami Hurricanes 41-14 in Tallahassee.
Photo By: Glenn Beil/Democrat

After throwing two interceptions in the first half, Winston was 12 of 14 for 164 yards in the second half. He looked every bit like the player that has captured the fanbase's attention through the first two months of the season.

"I was extremely proud of the way he dealt with that," Fisher said of Winston's first-half miscues. "That's a sign that you're growing. ... Heck, sometimes I forget he's a freshman."

Junior running back Devonta Freeman also had a big night for the Seminoles, finishing with 176 total yards and three scores.

"I think Devonta Freeman played his tail off," Fisher said. "That little guy – what a warrior."

As well as it ended, the first half was easily the worst of Winston's career. Which is to say, he looked human.

The redshirt freshman quarterback threw two interceptions that the Hurricanes turned into 14 points in an up-and-down first-half performance.

After leading the Seminoles on a 13-play, 72-yard TD march on the opening drive of the game, culminating in a five-yard Devonta Freeman touchdown run, he got the ball back after the Seminoles' defense forced a punt.

But on third down from his own 29, Winston badly overthrew Rashad Greene and was intercepted by Deon Bush at the Miami 35.

Five plays later the Hurricanes were in the end zone after Morris threw a perfect pass to Allen Hurns, who beat Williams for a 30-yard touchdown.

Winston and the Seminoles answered back

Kelvin Benjamin snares a Jameis Winston pass to set up a touchdown as Miami's A. J. Highsmith defends.
Photo By: Mike Ewen/Democrat

though, driving 79 yards in 11 plays to retake the lead.

The big plays on the drive were a 35-yard leaping grab by Kelvin Benjamin at the Miami 9 and then a Winston scramble inside the Hurricanes' 1. James Wilder Jr. scored on the next play and FSU was up 14-7.

It was 21-7 less than five minutes later when Freeman took a screen pass and raced untouched into the end zone for a 48-yard touchdown.

And when the Seminoles sent Miami backwards on the next series, thanks to a 14-yard sack by Mario Edwards Jr., it looked like Florida State had a chance to take control of the game right before the half.

But Winston missed tight end Nick O'Leary badly over the middle and was intercepted again.

And again the Hurricanes made the turnover pay, driving 57 yards in eight plays to cut the lead to 21-14 on a terrific catch by Hurns in the corner of the end zone – on a ball that was actually tipped by FSU safety Jalen Ramsey.

Winston finished the first half 9 of 15 for 161 yards, one touchdown, two interceptions and 33 yards rushing. But the Hurricanes had 14 points off his two turnovers to keep themselves in the game.

Florida State racked up 258 yards of total offense in the first half and was 6 of 7 on third down. Miami had 170 yards – with Morris throwing for 117 yards and two scores on 7 of 12 passing. But the two Winston interceptions loomed large over the first two quarters.

"He was telling us in the first half, 'We're all right, keep playing ball,'" FSU left tackle Cam Erving said of Winston. "He told us at halftime there are no more turnovers."

And there weren't.

The Seminoles' offense started the second half just like it did the first, marching down the field for another touchdown. Winston was 3 of 3 on the drive for 57 yards, including a 26-yarder to Kenny Shaw down to the Miami 5.

One play later, Wilder was diving into the end zone for a two-touchdown lead for the Seminoles.

And less than five minutes later, it was a 21-point advantage.

Williams got some retribution on Morris with an interception on a deep pass intended for freshman Stacy Coley, and then Winston drove the Seminoles 79 yards for yet another score.

Winston was 4 of 4 on the drive for 56 yards and Freeman finished off the march with a 12-yard touchdown run around the left side. It was the third TD of the night for the Miami native and all but iced the win for the Seminoles.

Roberto Aguayo added two fourth-quarter field goals to finish the scoring for Florida State, which has now scored 40 or more points in eight straight games, a new school record.

"We just dominated," Freeman said. "All my brothers did their right assignments. Coach Jimbo put us in great situations. The coaches prepared us well. We knew it was going to come down to the running game and we just had to be consistent."

BOX SCORE

FLORIDA STATE 41, MIAMI 14

Florida State	7	14	14	6	— 41
Miami	7	7	0	0	— 14

First Quarter
FS- 09:16 Devonta Freeman 5 yd run (Roberto Aguayo kick) 5:44 0
UM- 02:43 Allen Hurns 33 yd pass from Stephen Morris (Matt Goudis kick) ,1:38

Second Quarter
FS- 10:42 James Wilder Jr. 1 yd run (Roberto Aguayo kick) ,6:50
FS- 05:08 Devonta Freeman 48 yd pass from Jameis Winston (Roberto Aguayo kick), 2:35
UM- 00:22 Allen Hurns 14 yd pass from Stephen Morris (Matt Goudis kick), 1:43

Third Quarter
FS- 08:33 James Wilder Jr. 5 yd run (Roberto Aguayo kick), 4:42
FS- 03:41 Devonta Freeman 12 yd run (Roberto Aguayo kick), 4:38

Fourth Quarter
FS- 06:52 Roberto Aguayo 25 yd field goal , 6:19
FS- 01:03 FS Roberto Aguayo 28 yd field goal, 3:39

	UM	FSU
First downs	17	25
Rushes-yards	83	192
Passing	8	15
Comp-Att-Int	16-28-2	21-29-2
Fumbles-Lost	0-0	1-0
Penalties-Yards	2-5	6-55
Time of Possession	21:27	38:33

FSU FEATURE

COACH JIMBO FISHER

SENTIMENTAL REUNION
FISHER WILL ALWAYS HAVE FOND MEMORIES OF AUBURN DAYS

BY COREY CLARK

Just about every time the 1993 Florida State national championship season was brought up around Jimbo Fisher this season, he flashed a wide smile and reminded anyone in the room that there was only one undefeated team in the nation that year. And it wasn't the Seminoles.

It was the team he was preparing to play for the 2013 national championship.

While he's now the head coach at FSU, it's understandable that the 1993 Auburn Tigers football team would have a special place in Fisher's heart. After all, you never forget your first Division I-A coaching job. Or your first perfect season. And Auburn, Ala., is where Fisher got to experience both.

"Looking back now, I didn't even know what I didn't know," Fisher said with a laugh. "I was just going about it, just full force. I was kind of like a freshman. I was a I-AA coach. We had great success at Samford. But when

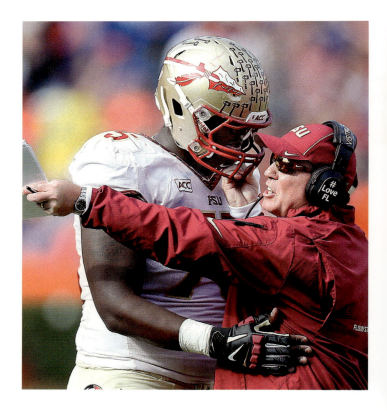

After being called for a penalty, Cameron Erving gets the attention of Coach Jimbo Fisher in the fourth quarter. FSU beat the Florida Gators 37-7 before a crowd of more than 90,000 fans at Ben Hill Griffin Stadium on Nov. 30, 2013.
Photo By: Mike Ewen/Democrat

Florida State quarterback Jameis Winston targets head Coach Jimbo Fisher with a cooler of water in the second half of the ACC Championship game against Duke in Charlotte, N.C. on Dec. 7, 2013. Florida State won 45-7. *Photo By: Chuck Burton/Democrat*

you go Division I at that level, major Division I football, it's a different deal.

"That's where I cut my teeth and learned how to coach and learned how to recruit. In the state of Alabama, you better know how to recruit and you better know how to handle your business. It's a great football state. I have nothing but great memories."

Fisher, who was 27 at the time, was brought to Auburn by Terry Bowden after serving as his offensive coordinator and quarterbacks coach at Samford.

It's almost hard for the FSU head coach to comprehend when he thinks back to those early coaching days. Fisher recently signed a new contract extension that is rumored to be worth more than $4 million per year. He is coaching the No. 1 team in the country, preparing to play Auburn in the BCS Championship game, and yet Fisher always seems to get sentimental when talking about his first stop on the crazy coaching carousel.

It was Samford, Ala., after all where he first met a young woman named Candi.

"I couldn't even pay rent," Fisher said with a smile. "That's why I had to start dating

Head Coach Jimbo Fisher leads his 2nd-ranked Seminoles onto the field against Wake Forest. The FSU Seminoles played like the No. 2 team in the nation by throttling the Wake Forest Demon Deacons 59-3 on a beautiful fall day in Winston Salem on Nov. 9, 2013. *Photo By: Mike Ewen/Democrat*

her. She had a job. I was just a poor football coach. We laugh about it sometimes. … I was the offensive coordinator and we went to the I-AA national semifinals and the I-AA quarterfinals and I made $15,000 a year.

"And you know what's funny? It was as happy as I ever was."

He then quickly added: "Not that I'm not happy now."

Now he's one of the most famous, most

Jimbo FIsher sends Jameis Winston out to attack the Bethune Cookman defense. FSU used a stifling defense, a potent running game and enough Jameis Winston passes to roll over the Bethune-Cookman Wildcats, 33-0, in the first half.
Photo By: Mike Ewen/Democrat

compensated coaches in the United States. In four years at Florida State, he's won two three bowl games, three ACC Atlantic Division titles, two conference championships and an Orange Bowl. His record overall at Florida State, before the championship, was 44-10. His record over the last 29 games was 27-2.

And as Fisher prepared for the 2013 championship, he was one win away from his second national championship ring (he got one as an assistant coach at LSU in 2003) and his second perfect season.

All he had to do was defeat the team that gave him that first perfect season, that first taste of major Division I-A football.

He says, ironically enough, that his current Florida State team reminds him of the Auburn one from two decades ago.

"That team had some great players that ended up being longtime NFL players," Fisher said. "Just like I think there will be a lot of those guys on our football team at Florida State. And it was a team back then that had a mission and an attitude. Our word back then was attitude.

"That team probably reminds more of this Florida State team than any team I've been around."

BB&T FIELD | NOVEMBER 9, 2013

FLORIDA STATE 59
WAKE FOREST 3

FLORIDA STATE LOOKING LIKE CLASS OF COLLEGE FOOTBALL

BY IRA SCHOFFEL

WINSTON-SALEM, N.C. — Well, that didn't take long.

Two days after Stanford knocked off Oregon and removed the suspense about whether an undefeated Florida State team might be locked out of the national championship game, the Seminoles annihilated another opponent and started a new conversation:

Are these guys the best team in the country?

That is something many of us who have followed this team have been wondering for weeks, but now it will get major traction nationally.

Here are some sample comments from media types on Twitter during the first quarter of FSU's game at Wake Forest.

"Let's see how Bama plays tonight, but FSU doing their best to prove they are the most complete team in CFB in 2013!!"

That was from ESPN's Kirk Herbstreit.

"FSU is obscene at the moment. I can't

Two young Jameis Winston fans show off their sign during the game. *Photo By: Mike Ewen/Democrat*

see anyone staying close until Pasadena."

That was from fellow ESPN broadcaster Scott Van Pelt.

These are the people who shape public opinion nationally, and they are jumping on the Seminoles' bandwagon with both feet.

Who could blame them?

Look at what Florida State has done during the last five games:

63-0 against then-No. 25 Maryland;

51-14 on the road against then-No. 3 Clemson;

Linebacker Christian Jones blindsides Wake Forest quarterback Tanner Price to force a fumble that was recovered by the Seminoles. *Photo By: Mike Ewen/Democrat*

49-17 against N.C. State;
41-14 against then-No. 7 Miami;
59-3 against Wake Forest.

Add it all up, and in their last five games — all against conference opponents — the Seminoles have romped to a 263-48 scoring margin. And they continue to find new ways to show off their supremacy.

Last week against Miami it was with dominance on the lines of scrimmage. In other games it has been the Jameis Winston show. This time, it was with a defensive mugging that was almost awe-inspiring.

They intercepted passes — a school-record tying six of them. They forced fumbles. They turned turnovers into touchdowns. They set the offense up for easy scores.

Remember how the Seminoles' offense produced all of those highlight-reel plays to take a 42-0 first-half lead against N.C. State? This time it was the defense doing the same exact thing.

Seriously. Think about that for a moment: In two of their last three games, the 'Noles have opened up 42-0 leads in the first half. Against conference opponents.

Wake Forest wide receiver Jared Crump got the ball stripped by Seminole defender Gerald Demps in the second half. The ball was ruled incomplete. *Photo By: Mike Ewen/Democrat*

Veteran Wake Forest head Coach Jim Grobe said all week that this looked like the best FSU team he has seen in his 13 years in the league, and he sounded more impressed after seeing the Seminoles in person.

"What's really an amazing thing — I told Jimbo (Fisher) before the game — you're talking about a football team that had 11 kids drafted last year. I mean that's unbelievable," Grobe said. "You look at this football team, and I think it's probably the best one we've faced since I've been at Wake Forest. And that's after they lost 11 guys to the NFL last year. So it's a pretty special football team."

Grobe went on to explain that it's not just the FSU talent that is so impressive; he said these Seminoles are as well-coached as any team he has seen in a long time.

And to think, until late Thursday night, many experts thought this team might be denied an opportunity to play for it all.

I personally never bought into that line of thinking. Even if Oregon and Alabama had run the table without a loss, I was convinced the Seminoles would have moved ahead of the Ducks eventually.

Things had been trending that way for weeks. Oregon kept winning, but the Seminoles kept closing the gap by taking their votes.

FSU running back Karlos Williams finds a hole during a second half run against the Demon Deacons in Winston Salem on Nov. 9, 2013.
Photo By: Mike Ewen/Democrat

I'm not so sure the Seminoles wouldn't have moved ahead of Oregon in the polls this week even if the Ducks had pulled off a late miracle victory against Stanford. At some point, the voters would have stopped holding themselves hostage by where they ranked teams in the preseason, and started rewarding the team performing at the highest level. And FSU is simply playing better than any team in college football.

Offense. Defense. Special teams.

They have it all.

Does that mean the Seminoles will bring home the crystal trophy? Are they definitely going to commemorate the 20th anniversary of the school's first national championship by winning one more?

There are no guarantees.

The pressure undoubtedly will mount in these next few weeks. Up until now, the 'Noles have had nothing to lose. They weren't picked to win a national title. They weren't picked to win their own division of the ACC.

They've had to fight and scrap for respect all season, and that's exactly how they've played.

Now, though, the praise is coming in waves. Seemingly overnight, these guys have gone from outsiders to sprinting down the inside track.

The question we have to ask is whether they can maintain the edge that has helped make them so dominant. Can they keep playing hungry when media and fans are trying to stuff them with compliments?

If they do, they just might win it all.

No one in college football is playing better.

And there's a good reason for that. I'm not sure any other team is capable.

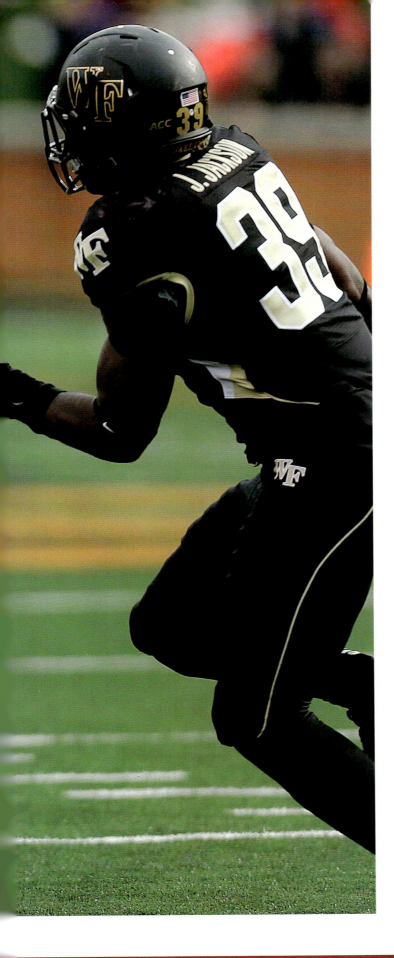

Jacob Coker tries to elude the rush of Wake Forest's Justin Jackson in the second half. The FSU Seminoles played like the No. 2 team in the nation by throttling the Wake Forest Demon Deacons 59-3 on a beautiful fall day in Winston Salem.
Photo By: Mike Ewen/Democrat

BOX SCORE

FLORIDA STATE 59, WAKE FOREST 3

FSU	21	21	10	7 —	59
Wake	0	0	0	3 —	3

First Quarter
FSU - James Wilder 5 run (Robert Aguayo kick), 7:15. Drive: 13-80, 5:48.
FSU - Devonta Freeman 1 run (Aguayo kick), 6:25. Drive: 2-2, 0:41.
FSU - Kelvin Benjamin 18 pass from Jameis Winston (Aguayo kick), 2:10. Drive: 2-15, 0:47.

Second Quarter
FSU - Nate Andrews 56 INT return (Aguayo kick), 14:15.
FSU - Jalen Ramsey 23 fumble recovery (Aguayo kick), 13:56.
FSU - Chad Abram 2 pass from Winston (Aguayo kick), 0:11. Drive: 8-57, 1:36.

Third Quarter
FSU - Karlos Williams 5 run (Aguayo kick), 12:03. Drive: 1-5, 0:07.
FSU - Aguayo 42 FG, 8:24.

Fourth Quarter
WF - Chad Hedlund 23 FG, 9:07.
FSU - Kermit Whitfield 97 kickoff return (Aguayo kick), 8:52.
Att. 30,856.

	Wake Forest	FSU
First downs	8	19
Rushes-yards	40-103	34-89
Passing	63	207
Comp-Att-Int	7-25-6	22-39-1
Return Yards	37	101
Punts-Avg.	9-41.0	6-38.8
Fumbles-Lost	1-1	3-1
Penalties-Yards	10-100	5-40
Time of Possession	31:02	28:58

FLORIDA STATE -VS- WAKE FOREST

DOAK CAMPBELL STADIUM | NOVEMBER 16, 2013

FLORIDA STATE 59
SYRACUSE 3

ORANGE CRUSHED
SYRACUSE BECOMES LATEST BLOWOUT VICTIM FOR NO. 2 'NOLES

BY COREY CLARK

This just isn't normal.

For the second week in a row, the No. 2 Florida State football team hammered an ACC opponent by the score of 59-3. For the ninth time in 10 games, the Seminoles won by at least four touchdowns. And it was the sixth time this season they've scored over 50.

Whether they're playing in front of 83,000 rabid fans in Death Valley, whether they're playing in front of 30,000 yawning fans at Wake Forest or whether they're playing three days after an allegation involving their star quarterback comes to light, it doesn't matter.

The 2013 Seminoles are simply steamrolling everyone.

"That's one thing Coach Fisher always talks about — stay on them," FSU quarterback Jameis Winston said. "We want to stay on them and when we're up big, just make it hurt."

For perspective, the last Division-I team to win consecutive games in which it scored at least 59 points and allowed three or

FSU fans came dressed for the massacre during their Homecoming game against the visiting Syracuse Orange.
Photo By: Mike Ewen/Democrat

FSU running back Devonta Freeman races for a first down as Syracuse defender Robert Walsh gives chase in the first quarter against the visiting Syracuse Orange. *Photo By: Mike Ewen/Democrat*

less? Florida State. In 1988.

So, no, the way the 10-0 Seminoles have jumped out on these teams — for the third time in four games Florida State has had a 35-0 lead early in the second quarter — is not normal.

"I respect how they do that," FSU head Coach Jimbo Fisher said. "We challenge them to do that. The way they're practicing and the way they're playing ... I respect that very much. That's why I say it's a fun group of guys to coach and be around."

If he was feeling any effects of the last week, Winston certainly didn't show it. The Heisman Trophy candidate completed his first 11 passes and finished the first half 19 of 21 for 277 yards and two touchdowns.

He didn't play a snap in the second half.

"We want to be elite," said Winston,

FSU's Kenny Shaw grimmaces as Syracuse defender Dyshawn Davis comes in for the tackle against the visiting Syracuse Orange.
Photo By: Mike Ewen/Democrat

who now has more TD passes on the season (28) than Heisman Trophy winner Charlie Ward (27) did in 1993. "We want to be great. And just when we had the '93 championship team come down, we want to be just like those guys. We want to keep everything moving the right way."

Florida State is now 10-0 on the season and wrapped up its first perfect ACC campaign since 2000. The Seminoles are also the first squad in conference history to score 40-plus points in 10 straight games.

And the history-making Seminoles were never threatened on Saturday as they completely obliterated the visiting Orange (5-5) from the start. Winston led a six-play, 77-yard drive on the opening series that culminated with a James Wilder Jr. 3-yard TD run.

Freshman speedster Kermit Whitfield scored on a 74-yard toss-sweep play on the next series, junior running back Devonta Freeman added a four-yard TD run, Rashad Greene caught a six-yard touchdown and Kelvin Benjamin followed with a six-yard TD catch of his own on a fade pass into the corner of the end zone.

When Roberto Aguayo connected on a career-long 53-yard field goal with 1:37 left, Florida State had itself a ho-hum 38-0 lead at the half. And the Seminoles had outgained the Orange 374 to 68.

From the opening kick, it was just an avalanche for the Orange, who finished with just 247 yards on 78 plays.

"That's one of the best football teams I've seen in my 23 years of coaching," Syracuse head coach Scott Shafer said. "They are big, they are fast, they are talented and they know what they're doing."

And as they've proven over the first 10 games of 2013, they do it no matter the circumstances.

"It's the way we prepare," said junior defensive tackle Timmy Jernigan, who had six tackles and one tackle for loss. "The way that we practice. Coach Fisher does a great job of just making practices tough and as hard as it possibly can be. ... I feel like we see a lot of stuff throughout the week, so the game doesn't really faze us."

Said Fisher: "Very proud of our guys. I thought we came out very focused, and again started very fast."

FSU's Jameis Winston escapes the tackle of Syracuse's Eric Crume in the first half. The FSU Seminoles used big plays on offense and a swarming defense to take a 38-0 lead into halftime during their Homecoming game against the visiting Syracuse Orange.
Photo By: Mike Ewen/Democrat

FSU receiver Rashad Greene snares a touchdown pass from Syracuse defenders Julian Whigham (21) and Jeremi Wilkes (28) in the first half. The FSU Seminoles took a 38-0 lead into halftime during their Homecoming game against the visiting Syracuse Orange.
Photo By: Mike Ewen/Democrat

BOX SCORE

FLORIDA STATE 59, SYRACUSE 3

Florida State	28	10	21	0	— 59
Syracuse	0	0	0	3	— 3

First Quarter
FS- 12:29 James Wilder Jr. 3 yd run (Roberto Aguayo kick), 2:31
FS - 10:41 Kermit Whitfield 74 yd run (Roberto Aguayo kick), 0:13
FS - 04:41 Devonta Freeman 4 yd run (Roberto Aguayo kick), 2:50
FS - 00:40 Rashad Greene 6 yd pass from Jameis Winston (Roberto Aguayo kick), 1:32

Second Quarter
FS - 11:52 Kelvin Benjamin 6 yd pass from Jameis Winston (Roberto Aguayo kick), 1:39
FS -05:07 Roberto Aguayo 53 yd field goal, 1:37

Third Quarter
FS - 10:51 James Wilder Jr. 37 yd run (Roberto Aguayo kick),1:15
FS -07:45 Nick O'Leary 17 yd pass from Sean Maguire (Roberto Aguayo kick), 1:31 0
FS -05:47 Chris Casher 31 yd fumble recovery (Roberto Aguayo kick)

Fourth Quarter
SU -07:42 Ryan Norton 32 yd field goal, 20-66 10:01

	SU	FSU
First downs	17	20
Rushes-yards	50-143	19-225
Passing	7	13
Comp-Att-Int	15-28-1	22-26-1
Return Yards	7	45
Punts-Avg.	7-40	2-48
Fumbles-Lost	0-0	1-31
Penalties-Yards	3-20	2-10
Time of Possession	41:42	18:18

DOAK CAMPBELL STADIUM | NOVEMBER 23, 2013

FLORIDA STATE 80
IDAHO 14

RECORD ROMP
SEMINOLES SET SCHOOL RECORD WITH 80 POINTS

BY COREY CLARK

Well, might as well break the single-game scoring record, too.

In a year when the Florida State football team is shattering school and conference marks seemingly every week, the Seminoles finished up the 2013 home schedule with even more as they crushed Idaho 80-14 on Saturday at Doak Campbell Stadium.

Not only did FSU break the ACC record for most points in a single season (currently at 607), but the 80 points on Saturday was the most a Florida State football team has ever scored in a game, breaking the previous record of 77 set by the 1995 team.

"I don't think our high school basketball team reached 80 points," said senior receiver Kenny Shaw, who had five catches for 107 yards and two touchdowns.

After the game head coach Jimbo Fisher was asked if he had ever been on a team that scored 80 points before.

"Yes," he said. "When I was in college (at Salem College in West Virginia) against Samford. My first game was against them. 82-9."

When told that his head coach had quar-

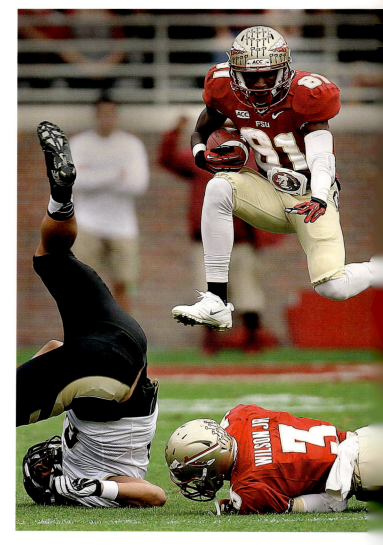

FSU senior Kenny Shaw leaps over Jesus Wilson after catching a pass during the opening moments of the first quarter. Shaw had more than 100 reception yards in the first half.
Photo By: Mike Ewen/Democrat

FSU fans had much to cheer about during the blowout victory over Idaho. FSU kept the pedal to the metal and took an 80-14 lead late into the second half. *Photo By: Mike Ewen/Democrat*

terbacked a team that scored 82 points, FSU freshman quarterback Jameis Winston smiled.

"Well, I mean, I guess we've got to step our game up," he said.

Winston finished 14 of 25 for 225 yards, four touchdowns and zero interceptions. He now has 32 TD passes on the year, which is one shy of Chris Weinke's school record set in 2000.

Winston is still in the midst of an investigation in which he is accused of sexual battery, but that outside turmoil certainly hasn't seemed to affect him very much – if at all — his past two games.

"The football field is a sanctuary to me," said Winston. "And it's like that for all my teammates. I can feel it. Because when we all go on that field everything is just zoned out. Clear the mechanism. And focus."

Apparently their focus on Saturday, like it has been every week this season, was to obliterate the opponent.

And this particular opponent was an Idaho team (1-10) that had no shot of staying on the field with FSU, which is the first team ever to score 40-plus points in its first 11 games of the season.

"I feel like we're playing at a high level,"

FSU's James Wilder Jr. races ahead of Idaho defenders enroute to a 49-yard gain in the second quarter. Wilder eventually scored a touchdown on the drive. The Florida State Seminoles used some big plays on the defense and a steady offensive attack to take a 42-7 lead into the half. *Photo By: Mike Ewen/Democrat*

said junior defensive tackle Timmy Jernigan, who had 4 ½ tackles for loss and 2 ½ sacks. "We've just got to keep playing at this level."

Very few teams in college football history have played at the level the 2013 Seminoles have through 11 games.

Florida State, which has now outscored its 11 opponents by a total margin of 607-125, was favored by 57 on Saturday. And covered rather easily.

The junior running back trio of Devonta Freeman (11 carries for 129 yards), Karlos Williams (10 for 114) and James Wilder (4 for 85) combined for 328 yards and four touchdowns on just 25 attempts.

Shaw and sophomore receiver Kelvin Benjamin each had two touchdown catches.

Linebacker Telvin Smith and linebacker E.J. Levenberry both had interception returns for scores as the Florida State defense had four interceptions overall.

"We could tackle better as a defense," Jernigan said. "There were a lot of missed tackles out there. So we've really got to make that up this week. As we go up against better football teams they're going to turn those into seven points. We've really got to tighten up."

Fisher didn't disagree. Even though his team put an 80 on the board and won by 66 points, he wasn't completely pleased with his team's performance either. Which says just how much of a mismatch Saturday really was.

"Solid performance," Fisher said. "I thought we were a little off in the first half. I thought we were more athletic, but I don't think we tackled well in the first half. I thought on offense we had some lapses, mental things, that we haven't had in a while.

"But we overcame them (and) made plays."

A lot of plays. Which led to a lot of points and yet another blowout win.

Florida State finishes up the regular season with a road trip to play the rival Florida Gators, who lost to Georgia Southern on Saturday.

"It's more of a pride game," Winston said. "It doesn't matter if we have everything to lose (and) they have nothing to lose. ... All of the other stuff, it doesn't really matter. They're going to play their best game when they play against us."

BOX SCORE

FLORIDA STATE 80, IDAHO 14

Idaho	0	7	0	7	—14
Florida State	21	21	17	21	—80

First Quarter
FS - 09:58 Devonta Freeman 60 yd run (Roberto Aguayo kick), 2:44
FS - 05:18 Kelvin Benjamin 32 yd pass from Jameis Winston (Roberto Aguayo kick), 2:02
FS - 03:05 Telvin Smith 79 yd interception return (Roberto Aguayo kick)

Second Quarter
FS - 12:48 Kenny Shaw 46 yd pass from Jameis Winston (Roberto Aguayo kick), 2:04
FS - 05:54 James Wilder Jr. 1 yd run (Roberto Aguayo kick), 1:33
UI - 00:41 Richard Montgomery 15 yd pass from Taylor Davis (Austin Rehkow kick), 1:44
FS - 00:04 Kenny Shaw 20 yd pass from Jameis Winston (Roberto Aguayo kick), 0:29

Third Quarter
FS - 13:11 Kelvin Benjamin 21 yd pass from Jameis Winston (Roberto Aguayo kick), 1:43
FS - 11:34 Karlos Williams 4 yd run (Roberto Aguayo kick), 0:47
FS - 03:07 Roberto Aguayo 42 yd field goal, 5:32

Fourth Quarter
FS - 14:25 Karlos Williams 25 yd run (Roberto Aguayo kick), 2:21
FS - 07:18 Ryan Green 2 yd pass from Sean Maguire (Roberto Aguayo kick), 1:20
FS - 04:19 E.J. Levenberry 78 yd interception return (Roberto Aguayo kick)
UI - 00:42 Najee Lovett 14 yd pass from Josh McCain (Austin Rehkow kick), 3:37

	UI	FSU
First downs	22	28
Rushes-yards	7-59	14-336
Passing	286	309
Comp-Att-Int	21-45-4	23-39-1
Return Yards	7-110-0	6-139-0
Punts-Avg.	8-48.6	1-40
Fumbles-Lost	0-0	1-1
Penalties-Yards	7-45	6-65
Time of Possession	32:32	26:46

FSU FEATURE

BRYAN STORK

SEMINOLES' DREAM CHASER

FSU'S STORK OVERCOMES PERSONAL TRAGEDY TO EXCEL ON FOOTBALL FIELD

BY COREY CLARK

Dreams are what drive Bryan Stork. They always have.

When he was little, when he first fell in love with football, he wanted to be Brett Favre.

As he grew older, and bigger, he dreamed of catching touchdown passes in Doak Campbell Stadium as a tight end.

After earning a scholarship to Florida State, he transformed his body into an offensive lineman who now dreams of having a long career in the NFL.

And after that, he says, he wants to buy a piece of farm land, with an air strip, so he can fly away anytime he wants.

These are the dreams that have shaped Stork. These are the dreams that have driven, and continue to drive, the starting center on Florida State's undefeated football team.

But there's another dream he had — just about 18 months ago — that will stay

Center Bryan Stork calls out a defender as the 8th-ranked Florida State Seminoles take down the Boston College Eagles 48-34 on Sept.28, 2013.
Photo By: Glenn Beil/Democrat

Jameis Winston celebrates with center Bryan Stork as the 5th-ranked Florida State Seminoles roll over the 3rd-ranked Clemson Tigers 51-14 on Oct. 19, 2013, at Memorial Stadium in Clemson, S.C. *Photo By: Glenn Beil/Democrat*

with him as long as he lives. It had nothing to do with private planes or riches or NFL fame. It was a just a conversation with his father. Who had passed away three years earlier.

PASSION FOR FOOTBALL

Larry Stork was a "daredevil," according to his youngest son.

"He always was skydiving," Bryan remembered. "He had like 350 jumps. Almost died three times. He was a pilot, too. I grew up flying planes with him."

When Bryan was little, about 8 years old, Larry would take him up in his small plane and let him fly. He would even let him pull back the throttle on takeoff.

"My dad showed me a lot of things at an early age that I think helped me mature a lot quicker," Stork said. "And I can't thank my dad enough for that. It's paying off."

Stork knows where he got his love for flying from, but he's not sure why he became so passionate about football. He said he thinks it started when his older brother joined the high school football team.

"I remember he brought over his helmet home one day to show me," said Bryan, who didn't live with his older half-siblings, Shane and Jenny. "I started putting it on, and was like, 'Wow, I like this.' I remember running around the yard and I just felt invincible."

Stork lived the first 12 years of his life in Illinois, where he became obsessed with the game.

He would throw passes at trees. Kick field goals through a make-shift goal post his dad had built for him. He had a few friends who would come over to play tackle football. But then that stopped rather abruptly.

"Because I was breaking all my friends' bones," Stork said.

So it was two-hand touch after that. But he didn't care. As long as he was playing.

When he was in middle school, Stork and his dad moved from the Midwest to Vero Beach. They lived by themselves as his mother stayed back in Illinois.

Not long after they arrived in Florida, Larry was diagnosed with cancer.

'FOUND MY WAY'

There's nothing that can adequately prepare a son for the loss of his father. Even if he knows the diagnosis. Even as he watches the disease — day after day, month after month and year after year — eat away at his father's body, it's still pure heartbreak when that last breath is taken.

Larry Stork died on Oct. 22, 2008. He was 55 years old.

Bryan was 17. A high school senior, who was now living in a house by himself.

"I remember dad was worried about me," Stork said. "I wasn't the best student. I had a knack for breaking stuff, like any teenager does, and I just somehow found my way. Somebody upstairs was looking out for me or something. I don't know.

"He had been sick for like five years, so I understood how to take care of the house, how to cook ... I did it all."

He did it with the help of his sister, Jenny Wright, who had moved about five miles away with her own family.

Jenny would pay the bills, help do laundry, and even come by the house after she got her own kids ready for school each morning. Half the time, when she got there, her younger brother was already gone.

Bryan wasn't just getting to school on time each day, without any adult supervision, he was getting there early.

"He always did what he was supposed to do," Jenny said. "I really didn't have to push him to do anything. He said, 'Dad just went peacefully, he didn't complain. So why can't I get out there and do this for him?'"

She added with a laugh: "I think he was scared of Dad haunting him or something."

"I just knew what I had at stake," Stork said. "I always felt like deep down inside I could do something very special with my life. And I just felt if I stayed true and kept doing things right, things would work out. I know a lot of people were worried about me."

His sister most of all.

She knew he had just suffered a trag-

Bryan Stork looks to throw a block as Florida State dominates the Pittsburgh Panthers at Heinz Field in Pittsburgh, Pa., during the team's first game of the 2013 football season.
Photo By: Glenn Beil/Democrat

Jameis Winston and center Bryan Stork yell out plays as they survey the defense. FSU used a stifling defense, a potent running game and enough Winston passes to roll over the Bethune-Cookman Wildcats, 33-0, in the first half on Sept. 21, 2013.
Photo By: Mike Ewen/Democrat

edy. They both had. But while Jenny was in her mid-20s, with a family of her own, Bryan was still in high school. Living in a house by himself. Trying to gain weight for football (he weighed just 220 pounds the fall of his senior year), trying to raise his grades so he would be eligible to play at Florida State.

All the while still trying to grasp the loss of their father.

She couldn't imagine that kind of stress at 17.

"He really put all of his anger, his hurt, he put it all into football," Jenny said. "I think that's what kept him going. I don't know. Bryan's a tough kid to figure out. He's always just kind of kept it in. ... It was always me talking. It took me to talk to him to get him to open up and talk to me about what was going on in his head.

"We spent a lot of nights up late, just talking. Sometimes we'd sit there and cry and then say, 'Well, Dad wouldn't want you crying.' But we leaned on each other a lot."

Now she's overjoyed at what has become of her "little" brother.

"I'm so, so proud of him," Jenny said. "I want him to go as far as he can go. I'm definitely a proud sister."

ONE LAST VISIT

At 6-foot-4, 300 pounds, Bryan Stork is the anchor on one of the nation's best offensive lines. On perhaps the nation's best team. And when this season is over, he has a chance to make a living playing the sport he has loved since that day he first put on his brother's football helmet.

"He's a great center," FSU quarterback Jameis Winston said. "And people look at Bryan and say, 'Oh, he's quiet.' But Bryan is a really funny guy. We have a good relationship because Bryan accepts whoever you are. He doesn't judge anybody.

"He's just a great person. And he's a great center. The center-quarterback relationship has to be great and I love my center."

With all of Stork's success at the college level, with all of the starts and all of the wins, he gets told constantly by friends and family, "if only your dad could see you now."

"And I'm like, he does see me," Stork said. "He sees through me."

Which brings us back to that dream.

Stork doesn't remember the exact date Larry came to visit his subconscious, only that it was about a "year and a half ago."

But the son remembers the conversation in such vivid detail that it has become a cherished memory with his father.

"I told him all my stories about college," Stork said. "Who I used to date, who I didn't. What me and my buddies did. I told him about this game. Or that game. The time we beat Florida here. And we had this come-to-peace meeting.

"We were just sitting there. The two of us. Drinking our Bud Lights. And just chilling."

For a fleeting moment, they were back together again. The cancer was gone. It felt so natural, so real, that for Stork it might as well have been a real conversation. One last man-to-man talk between father and son.

"It was really weird," he said. "And I haven't had a dream about him since.

"I would give anything for him to be back here, but I know he's not in pain anymore. He's in heaven. And that's what's best."

BEN HILL GRIFFIN STADIUM | NOVEMBER 30, 2013

FLORIDA STATE 37
FLORIDA 7

STOMP IN THE SWAMP

FSU WRAPS UP UNDEFEATED REGULAR SEASON WITH WIN

BY COREY CLARK

GAINESVILLE — It was the perfect end to a perfect regular season.

Like they have all year long, the No. 2 Florida State Seminoles dominated their opponent on Saturday afternoon. This one just happened to be the Florida Gators. In the Swamp. In front of 90,454 fans who watched as FSU rolled to a 37-7 victory.

"That's what we expect to do," Florida State defensive tackle Timmy Jernigan said. "With the talent we have on this team, and the coaches we have on this staff, we expect to go out and dominate on Saturdays. We don't accept nothing less."

It's just the fourth undefeated regular season in program history and by far the most dominant, as the Seminoles beat every team on the schedule by at least 14 points and 11 of the 12 by at least 27.

They will take on 10-2 Duke on Saturday night in Charlotte, N.C., in the ACC Championship Game.

FSU is also expected to move to No. 1 in the polls today following Auburn's stunning, 34-28, win over Alabama on Saturday.

The fourth-ranked Tigers returned a last-second missed field goal for a touchdown to knock off the top-ranked Crimson Tide in the Iron Bowl.

FSU was last ranked No. 1 in the Associated Press poll on Oct. 1, 2000.

"I am very proud of this group," FSU head Coach Jimbo Fisher said. "Because they played one game at a time. It never left their head. It doesn't worry about the results, it doesn't worry about the outcome, it doesn't worry about what we have in front of us.

"It's just a very mature group."

With a whole bunch of really good players.

Freshman quarterback Jameis Winston was 19 of 31 for 327 yards, three touchdowns and one interception. And all three TD passes went to sophomore Kelvin Benjamin, who had a career day with nine catches for 212 yards.

"We have so many weapons," Winston said. "Like, they had a linebacker on Nick O'Leary. Come on, man."

The Florida State offense actually strug-

Right: Seminole players gather to hoist the Gator head after beating their arch rivals. FSU beat the Florida Gators 37-7 before a crowd of more than 90,000 fans. FSU used its suffocating defense and some big throws by Jameis Winston to take a 17-0 lead into the half at Ben Hill Griffin Stadium.
Photo By: Mike Ewen/Democrat

FSU receiver Rashad Greene snares a first-down catch in front of Gator defender Jaylen Watkins in the fourth quarter.
Photo By: Mike Ewen/Democrat

gled for the first quarter and a half against the talented Gators, but went on a game-changing, 96-yard march to take a 10-0 lead late in the second quarter.

Winston found Kenny Shaw for 27 yards on third-and-25 and then Benjamin scored his first TD of the day when he caught a slant pass and bulled, fought and spun his way through the entire Florida secondary for a 45-yard TD.

Before that drive, Winston said he talked to the entire offense.

"Look, listen guys," Winston said. "This is going to define this game right here. If we can just shove it down their throats, this drive, 96 yards, we will win this football game."

He wasn't lying.

After the FSU defense forced another three-and-out (Florida had just eight first downs in the game), Winston found Benjamin again for a 29-yard TD to give FSU a 17-0 lead with 25 seconds left in the half.

It was obvious, senior center Bryan Stork said, that the Florida defense was gassed by the end of the first half – with many Gators putting hands on their hips in between plays.

"That's a sign of weakness," Stork said. "We saw it in the first quarter, second quarter. No disrespect to those guys. Those guys played hard. But, like I said, we're in good shape. We train hard."

On the other side of the ball, the Florida State defense was on a mission to stop the Gators' ground game. In last year's 37-26 win in Tallahassee, Florida rushed for 244 yards.

On Saturday, the Gators managed 78 yards on 24 attempts. And 50 of those came on one rush from Trey Burton in the first half.

"We definitely took it personally that they thought we were soft," said sophomore defensive end Mario Edwards, who caused a turnover on the Gators' first play of the second half with a sack and caused fumble.

Freshman kicker Roberto Aguayo connected from 40 yards out to give the Seminoles a 20-0 lead.

Junior running back Devonta Freeman made it 27-0 four minutes later with an 11-yard TD run – on the heels of Benjamin's 56-yard catch – and the only question remaining was how bad the final score would be.

Aguayo finished off the scoring with a 28-yard field goal and the Seminoles celebrated their largest margin of victory ever at Florida Field.

It was a complete 180-degree turnaround for fifth-year seniors like Stork, whose first time in Gainesville was for Tim Tebow's Senior Day in 2009 – when the undefeated Gators rolled over the Seminoles by 27 points.

Saturday was a bit different.

"I just remember being in shock," Stork said of that first trip to Gainesville. "But you mature. You grow older and go do it just like they did. Those were the dark days of Florida State, I always call them. We didn't have that good of a decade. I'm just happy it's in my control somewhat. It's in our control now."

If the No. 2 Seminoles can beat Duke on Saturday for their second straight ACC Championship, they'll be heading to Pasadena to play in the BCS Championship game. Either way, he and his teammates can savor the fact that they just finished the first perfect Florida State regular season since 1999.

"I'm pretty happy about that," Stork said. "It's cool. But you can't ever be satisfied. Ever."

FSU's Kelvin Benjamin makes a leaping catch in the game against the Florida Gators.
Photo By: Glenn Beil/Democrat

A NEW NO. 1

FSU MOVES TO TOP OF POLLS, BCS RANKINGS

BY IRA SCHOFFEL

It took Florida State's football team 13 years, including the last four under head Coach Jimbo Fisher, to make its way back to the top of the college football world.

Shortly after noon on Sunday, it became official.

After blowing out rival Florida, 37-7, and watching defending national champion Alabama fall at Auburn on Saturday, the Seminoles moved up one spot to No. 1 in both the Associated Press Top 25 and the USA Today Coaches Poll.

Sunday evening, they were granted the No. 1 spot in the BCS rankings.

But keeping with the philosophy that has helped them stay focused all season, FSU head Coach Jimbo Fisher said the Seminoles aren't about to start celebrating just yet. He said his coaches and players don't feel any differently now — as the nation's top-ranked team — than they did earlier in the season.

"No, not one bit," Fisher said during Sunday's ACC Championship Game media teleconference.

As soon as the Seminoles put the finishing touches on their 12-0 regular season this past weekend, their attention immediately moved to Saturday's conference title game against Duke.

Win that game, and the Seminoles will earn an invitation to the BCS national championship game in Pasadena, Calif. Lose it, and the No. 1 national ranking will be short-lived.

"I'm not worried about what we're ranked and what we're doing," Fisher said. "That'll all take care of itself. What we need to focus on is preparing for a great game this week and playing a great game against Duke. Whether you're (number) 1, 2, 3, 4, 5, whatever, it has no bearing on what we have

E.J. Levenberry rushes out to the Swamp. FSU used its suffocating defense and some big throws by Jameis Winston to take a 17-0 lead into the half at Ben Hill Griffin Stadium before a vocal Gator crowd. *Photo By: Mike Ewen/Democrat*

to do this week."

FSU, which last sported a No. 1 national ranking in October 2000, received 58 of 60 first-place votes in the AP Top 25, and 58 of 62 first-place votes from the coaches.

The Seminoles also were the clear-cut No. 1 in the BCS standings, which take into account the coaches' poll, the Harris Poll and several computer rankings. FSU had an average BCS ranking of .995, followed by No. 2 Ohio State (.950) and Auburn (.923).

There will be some debate this week, however, about which team should get to face the Seminoles for the national title, assuming FSU gets past the Blue Devils.

Ohio State is undefeated heading into the Big Ten Championship Game against Michigan State, while Auburn has one loss but knocked off Alabama and has other impressive wins.

"I think Florida State's the best team with flying colors," ESPN analyst David Pollack said during the BCS countdown show Sunday night. "I've thought Florida State was the best team the last several weeks ... the athletes that they have, to go with the level of dominance.

"And I think Auburn's the second-best team."

But ESPN's Kirk Herbstreit said he is convinced Ohio State will hold onto the No. 2 spot as long as it knocks off the Spartans this weekend.

FSU, meanwhile, is favored by 29 points in the ACC title game. And Fisher said a key to their success again will be blocking out the distractions, including this new top ranking.

"Hopefully we can do it one more week until the bowl season starts," he said.

"We've been able to focus and do that, not pay attention to the outside things and worry about anything. We can't worry about where we're ranked and what goes on. We've just got to worry about preparing and playing, and that's all we tell our guys, and hopefully we can do that at least one more week right here."

BOX SCORE

FLORIDA STATE, 37
FLORIDA, 7

FSU	3	14	10	10 —	37
UF	0	0	0	7 —	7

First Quarter
FSU - Robert Aguayo 49 FG, 3:43. Drive: 8-35, 4:00.

Second Quarter
FSU - Kelvin Benjamin 45 pass from Jameis Winston (Aguayo kick), 4:24. Drive: 12-96, 5:51.
FSU - Benjamin 29 pass from Winston (Aguayo kick), 0:25. Drive: 6-74, 1:42.

Third Quarter
FSU - Aguayo 40 FG, 11:02. Drive: 6-16, 2:36.
FSU - Devonta Freeman 11 run, 7:08. Drive: 5-84, 1:43.

Fourth Quarter
UF - Hunter Joyer 5 pass from Skyler Mornhinweg (francisco Velez kick), 13:39. Drive: 14-83, 8:29.
FSU - Benjamin 4 pass from Winston (Aguayo kick), 8:06. Drive: 10-79, 5:33.
FSU - Aguayo 28 FG, 3:14. Drive: 6-21, 3:38.
Att. 90,454.

	FSU	UF
First downs	20	8
Rushes-yards	32-129	24-78
Passing	327	115
Comp-Att-Int	19-31-1	20-25-0
Return Yards	24	125
Punts-Avg.	2-43.5	6-44.2
Fumbles-Lost	0-0	3-2
Penalties-Yards	6-55	6-45
Time of Possession	31:09	28:51

ACC CHAMPIONSHIP GAME

BANK OF AMERICA STADIUM | DECEMBER 7, 2013

FLORIDA STATE 45
DUKE 7

ONE TITLE DOWN

WINSTON, FSU WIN ACC; BCS GAME UP NEXT

BY COREY CLARK

CHARLOTTE, N.C — The Florida State Seminoles will play for the national championship.

Coming into Saturday night, they knew if they beat No. 20 Duke in the ACC Championship Game they would earn a spot in the BCS title game. So No. 1 FSU went out and did exactly that, scorching the Blue Devils 45-7 at the Bank of America stadium in Charlotte.

Florida State, which improved to 13-0 on the season, will likely play Auburn in the BCS Championship game on Jan. 6 in Pasadena, Calif. The matchup will be officially announced tonight on ESPN.

"It's surreal. We finally got it. It's a blessing," FSU receiver Kenny Shaw said of the expected news. "We ain't done yet. Nothing's changed."

FSU's Timmy Jernigan says he's impressed by the Tigers.

"They have a great football team," Jernigan said. "I've watched them and they play hard and they're nasty. We definitely will have to bring our 'A' game."

ACC Commissioner John Swofford presents the ACC Championship trophy to Jimbo Fisher, right, after the Seminoles crushed Duke 45-7 to take the ACC Championship in Charlotte, N.C, on Dec. 7, 2013.
Photo By: Glenn Beil/Democrat

The 13 wins are a school-record for the Seminoles and the ACC title is the 14th in program history.

Unlike virtually every other game this season though, Saturday night's win

Cameron Erving holds the ACC trophy as Seminole players celebrate after crushing Duke 45-7 to take the ACC Championship.
Photo By: Glenn Beil/Democrat

wasn't one of those typical FSU bludgeonings from start to finish. The beating took a while to get started.

The Seminoles didn't score in the first quarter for the first time all year and had just a 7-0 lead late in the second quarter. But junior running back Karlos Williams destroyed a Duke defender at the goal-line on a 12-yard TD run with 3:37 left. And Roberto Aguayo nailed a 45-yard field goal with 25 seconds left to give FSU a 17-0 lead at intermission.

Quarterback Jameis Winston, the overwhelming favorite to win the Heisman Trophy next week, had one of his worst halves of the season on Saturday night. And yet he was still 12 of 21 for 171 yards and a 14-yard TD pass to Kelvin Benjamin.

He finished with 330 yards.

"Watching him over whole season is amazing. I'm so happy he's my quarterback," FSU running back Karlos Williams said of Winston.

The redshirt freshman was intercepted at midfield on the penultimate drive of the first half and Duke had a chance to stay in the game late in the second quarter. But the Florida State defense did what it did all half long – it forced a three-and-out – and the Seminoles drove 53 yards in seven plays to set up Aguayo's field goal.

In total, Duke had eight possessions in the first half and seven were three-and-outs. Florida State All-American Lamarcus Joyner also intercepted Duke quarterback Anthony Boone at the FSU 22 after Jamison Crowder's 40-yard punt return set up the Blue Devils in FSU territory.

Even with Joyner's pick, though, Duke won the turnover battle in the first half. Not only did Winston throw the interception in the second quarter, but the Seminoles' first drive was halted when Devonta Freeman fumbled at the Duke 3-yard line.

And yet, even with the uneven first half from the FSU offense, the Seminoles still outgained the Blue Devils 268-94 in total yardage.

On Duke's first drive of the second half things got even worse for the Blue Devils. Boone was hit by freshman defensive back Nate Andrews while he was releasing the pass and senior linebacker Telvin Smith intercepted it.

Three plays later, Winston found Kenny Shaw for an 11-yard TD over the middle and the Seminoles were up 24-0. And after another Duke three-and-out, FSU drove 87 yards in the blink of an eye, with the last 57 coming on a Winston-to-Benjamin catch-and-run into the end zone.

That 31-0 lead became a 38-0 lead moments later. The Seminoles forced another turnover and Winston led another touchdown – this time doing the honors himself with a 17-yard run around left end.

Freeman then finished off the scoring with a 7-yard TD run up the middle. The junior running back had 18 carries for 91 yards, while Winston finished off his historical regular season with a 330-yard passing performance. He also added 59 yards rushing for the Seminole starters, who gained 562 yards in the win.

FSU's Jameis Winston leaps into the end zone for a touchdown during the ACC Championship game.
Photo By: Glenn Beil/Democrat

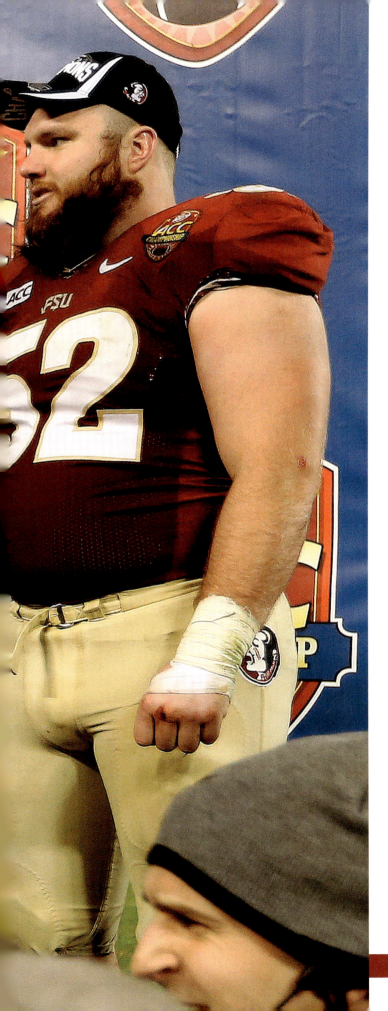

Jameis Winston does a little dance on stage after the Seminoles crushed Duke 45-7 to take the ACC Championship in Charlotte, N.C, on Dec. 7, 2013.
Photo By: Glenn Beil/Democrat

BOX SCORE

FLORIDA STATE 45, DUKE 7

Duke	0	0	0	7 —	7
Florida State	0	17	21	7 —	45

Second Quarter
FS -12:36 Jameis Winston pass complete to Kelvin Benjamin for 14 yards for a TOUCHDOWN. Roberto Aguayo extra point GOOD.
FS- 3:37 Karlos Williams rush for 12 yards for a TOUCHDOWN. Roberto Aguayo extra point GOOD.
FS- 0:25 Roberto Aguayo 45 yard field goal GOOD

Third Quarter
FS - 9:52 Jameis Winston pass complete to Kenny Shaw for 11 yards for a TOUCHDOWN. Roberto Aguayo extra point GOOD
FS -06:31 Jameis Winston pass complete to Kelvin Benjamin for 54 yards for a TOUCHDOWN. Roberto Aguayo extra point GOOD.
FS- 2:38 Jameis Winston rush for 17 yards for a TOUCHDOWN. Roberto Aguayo extra point GOOD.

Fourth Quarter
FS -07:25 Devonta Freeman rush for 7 yards for a TOUCHDOWN. Roberto Aguayo extra point GOOD.
DU- 01:01 Josh Snead rush for 5 yards for a TOUCHDOWN. Ross Martin extra point GOOD.

	Duke	FSU
First downs	16	30
Rushes-yards	31-99	43-239
Passing	140	330
Comp-Att-Int	21-42-2	19-32-2
Return Yards		
Punts-Avg.		
Fumbles-Lost	1	1
Penalties-Yards	3-32	6-65
Time of Possession	30:44	28:58

FSU FEATURE

JAMEIS WINSTON

ANOTHER BLOWOUT
FSU'S WINSTON WINS HEISMAN WITH 668 FIRST-PLACE VOTES

BY IRA SCHOFFEL

Florida State Seminoles quarterback Jameis Winston poses for a photo after being awarded the 2013 Heisman Trophy at the Marriott Marquis in New York City on Dec. 14, 2013.
Photo By: Adam Hunger-USA TODAY Sports

NEW YORK — So, this is what Jameis Winston meant by doing it big.

Florida State's phenomenal freshman quarterback, who smashed school, ACC and national records while leading the Seminoles to a perfect regular season and a spot in the national championship game, won the 2013 Heisman Trophy in a landslide Saturday night.

With his trademark gold necklace resting beneath the collar of a dark blue suit, Winston hugged his parents and teared up after the announcement was made live on ESPN.

Winston, who learned just over a week ago that he will not face charges following a sexual battery investigation, said his emotions got the best of him when he looked into the eyes of his mother and father, Loretta and Antonor Winston.

"They felt so proud," Winston explained later. "I ain't seen that look in their eyes in a long time. ... When you see your mom and you see your dad – when they've

Florida State Seminoles quarterback and 2013 Heisman Trophy winner Jameis Winston and Seminoles head Coach Jimbo Fisher pose with the trophy during a press conference at the New York Marriott Marquis Times Square following the awards ceremony.
Photo By: Brad Penner-USA TODAY Sports

been struggling through this whole process – and now you see that smile on their face, it comforted me."

The clear-cut voting was a fitting salute to a season's worth of blowouts for Winston and the No. 1 Florida State Seminoles.

The redshirt freshman received 668 of 900 first-place votes. Runner-up A.J. McCarron of Alabama was next with 79, followed by Northern Illinois quarterback Jordan Lynch (40), Boston College running back Andre Williams (29), Texas A&M quarterback Johnny Manziel (30) and Auburn running back Tre Mason (31).

Manziel, who won the 2012 Heisman Trophy, told reporters that even he voted for Winston.

While poise under pressure has been one of Winston's greatest characteristics on the field, the Seminoles' young star said he had a difficult time regaining his composure once his name was announced as the winner.

"When I went up there, I was like, 'I'm speechless,'" Winston said. "I don't have anything to say."

So instead of walking directly to the podium, he bought time by shaking hands with several former Heisman Trophy winners lined up along the back of the stage.

"I ended up shaking people's hands twice because I didn't know what to do," Winston laughed later.

It was an emotional night for Winston's head coach as well.

Jimbo Fisher, sitting in the audience

Florida State Seminoles quarterback and 2013 Heisman Trophy winner Jameis Winston kisses the trophy during a press conference at the New York Marriott Marquis Times Square. Photo By: Brad Penner-USA TODAY Sports

at the Best Buy Theater in Times Square, wiped away tears as Winston delivered a passionate, personal speech that touched on his first youth sports championship, his father losing his job three years ago, and a difficult last month that ended with the state attorney deciding there was not enough evidence to prove a crime occurred.

"When you watch someone work so hard for something — and be so team-oriented, not individual-oriented — it really reinforces that the good things happen to the good guys," Fisher said, noting that Winston never let the off-the-field drama get in the way of his teammates' goals.

"Just to know what he went through to get up there on that stage ... sometimes as a coach, it just hits you."

At just 19, Winston becomes the youngest winner of the Heisman Trophy. He joins a pair of former Seminoles who have interesting distinctions of their own – 2000 winner Chris Weinke is the oldest to have earned the award, and 1993 winner Charlie Ward is the only one to play in the NBA.

The voting was not without controversy.

Of the 900 Heisman voters who cast ballots, 115 left Winston off completely, leading to speculation that some penalized him because of the criminal allegation.

"God bless them," Winston said. "Obviously everyone has their own opinion. It's basically a numbers game. And I was blessed that I had the majority vote."

It was much more than that. According to Heisman officials, Winston's margin of victory — he had 2,205 total points, compared to 704 for McCarron — was the fifth-largest disparity of the last 50 years.

Winston, who didn't even win FSU's starting job until preseason camp, emerged on the Heisman scene in October when ESPN's cameras captured his inspirational pregame talk before the Seminoles took on then-No. 3 Clemson in a pivotal road game.

"If we're gonna do it then," Winston shouted that night, "we do it big!"

Over the next three hours, Winston proved to the world he had athletic talent to match his charisma. Playing before a raucous crowd in "Death Valley," Winston passed for 444 yards and led the Seminoles to a 51-14 victory. From there, it was blowout after blowout.

With one game remaining — the Jan. 6 national championship game against Auburn — Winston already has shattered several individual records. But as he has done throughout the season, Winston stressed on Saturday that the Heisman is a team award.

"This is not for me," he said. "This is for Florida State. This is for my team. Because if I didn't have those guys, I wouldn't even be here."

In an interview before the announcement, Winston told reporters that he and his teammates are, "trying to bring that late-'90s and the early-'90s swag back to Tallahassee."

He later was asked what he is going to tell his teammates when he returns to campus.

"This Heisman Trophy is ours," Winston said. "But that crystal ball will have OUR name on it."

Florida State Seminoles quarterback and 2013 Heisman Trophy winner Jameis Winston strikes a Heisman pose while holding the trophy during a press conference at the New York Marriott Marquis Times Square.
Photo By: Brad Penner-USA TODAY Sports

BCS CHAMPIONSHIP GAME

ROSE BOWL STADIUM | JANUARY 6, 2014

FLORIDA STATE 34
AUBURN 31

SEMINOLES RALLY FOR DRAMATIC VICTORY

WINSTON TOSSES 2-YARD TD PASS TO BENJAMIN WITH 13 SECONDS REMAINING

BY COREY CLARK

PASADENA, Calif — Jameis Winston already held legendary status at Florida State, becoming the youngest Heisman Trophy winner in college football history. On Jan. 6, 2014, he cemented his legacy with the drive of a lifetime.

Trailing by four, with 1:11 left, Winston drove the Seminoles 80 yards in 56 seconds, finishing off this instant classic of a championship game with a 2-yard TD pass to Kelvin Benjamin with 13 seconds left.

And when the Florida State defense stopped Auburn on its next two plays, the Seminoles had won the 2013 national championship 34-31.

"We have a tremendous football team," FSU Coach Jimbo Fisher said.

"This team has heart, guts and determination. It was an unbelievable win. I am going to tell you what. There's a lot of heart and guts down in Tallahassee, too. I said this from day one in spring ball. This team is spe-

Ronald Darby knocks the ball away from Auburn receiver Sammie Coates as Florida State and Auburn meet for the BCS National Championship game on Jan. 6, 2014.
Photo By: Glenn Beil/Democrat

Joseph Hernandez celebrates after Florida State defeats Auburn 34-31 to take the BCS National Championship game on Jan. 6, 2014. *Photo By: Glenn Beil/Democrat*

cial. They wanted to be an elite team."

Winston was 6 of 7 on the final drive, including a 49-yard catch and run by junior wideout Rashad Greene (nine catches for 147 yards) that set up the game-winning score. Florida State not only won its third national championship in program history in front of 94,208 in Pasadena, but it stopped the SEC's streak of seven straight titles.

"This is the best football game he played," Fisher said of Winston, who turned 20 on game day.

"Because he struggled for three quar-

ters. Great players understand great moments."

The Seminoles finish the season 14-0, while Auburn drops to 12-2.

And in a game that was sluggish for the first three quarters, the final quarter was one, long roller-coaster ride.

"We didn't lose faith, we didn't stop believing," FSU's Christian Jones said.

Added Rashad Greene: "We can take a punch. We showed we can take a punch and we can punch back."

The final quarter started with a Win-

FSU fans cheer at AJ Sports Bar & Grill in Tallahassee during the Championship game on Jan. 6, 2014.
Photo By: Michael Schwarz/Democrat

Above: Kelvin Benjamin picks up a first down as Florida State defeats Auburn 34-31 to take the BCS National Championship game on Jan. 6, 2014 at the Rose Bowl in Pasadena, Calif. *Photo By: Glenn Beil/Democrat*

Left: Rashad Greene picks up an early first down as Florida State and Auburn meet for the BCS National Championship Game on Jan. 6, 2014. The Noles struggled in the first half, but turned things around in the final minutes of the game for a 34-31 win over Auburn. *Photo By: Glenn Beil/Democrat*

ston incompletion and a punt. But FSU sophomore cornerback P.J. Williams gave the Seminoles life with an interception and the offense wasted little time taking advantage.

Winston hit Benjamin for a 20-yard gain and then found fullback Chad Abram in the flat for an 11-yard TD pass. The Seminoles would have wanted to go for two, but Devonta Freeman was called for an unsportsmanlike penalty after the TD and Fisher elected to go for the extra point, which Roberto Aguayo made from 35 yards out.

Still, the Seminoles had cut the lead to 21-20 and had all the momentum with almost an entire quarter still to play.

Auburn was able to steal some of it back with a long, methodical drive that got inside the FSU 10. But the Tigers couldn't convert on third down and had to settle for a field goal and a 24-20 lead.

It didn't stay that way for long.

Florida State freshman Kermit Whitfield, one of the fastest high school sprinters in the country in 2012, fielded the ensuing kick in his own end zone. Took off down the middle of the field, cut left, and then outraced

the Auburn coverage team for a 100-yard touchdown return and a 27-24 lead with four minutes remaining.

The Seminoles had their first lead since it was 3-0. But Auburn was able to answer right back, taking advantage of a defense that had been on the field for almost the entire fourth quarter.

Nick Marshall found Sammie Coates for an enormous completion on third down, after spinning out of a sack, and then Tre Mason bounced off two FSU defenders and scored on a 37-yard run with 1:19 left, setting up Winston's final drive of the 2013 season.

It was a remarkable performance for the All-American QB because he wasn't sharp for long stretches. But when it mattered most he was, throwing two TD passes in the fourth quarter and finishing with 237 yards passing.

And it was also a remarkable comeback for a Florida State team that hadn't been challenged all season. The Seminoles actually trailed 21-3 in the second quarter before mounting a furious rally.

The nation's leading scoring offense was held TD-less for the first 28 minutes of the game and the nation's leading scoring defense gave up 21 points and 232 yards of total offense.

Winston struggled mightily in the first half, completing just 6 of 15 passes for 62 yards. And his second-quarter fumble in his own territory led to Auburn's third touchdown.

Giorgio Newberry celebrates as Florida State defeats Auburn 34-31 to take the BCS National Championship game on Monday Jan. 6, 2014. The Florida State Seminoles used late-game heroics to take down the Auburn Tigers at the Rose Bowl in Pasadena, Calif.
Photo By: Glenn Beil/Democrat

Florida State actually took the lead to start the game when Winston engineered a nine-play, 59-yard drive, highlighted by a 29-yard completion to Greene on third and 16. Freshman Aguayo connected on a 35-yard field goal and the Seminoles led 3-0 just five minutes into the game.

The next 20 minutes of game time were a nightmare for Florida State, however.

It started when Auburn punter Steven Clark downed a punt at the FSU 2. Three plays later the Seminoles were punting and Chris Davis returned Cason Beatty's kick to the Florida State 25-yard line.

Auburn quarterback Nick Marshall then hit running back Tre Mason for a 12-yard TD pass and just like that Florida State trailed for the first time since September.

The Tigers scored again on their next drive when Marshall hit a wide open Melvin Ray, a Tallahassee native, for a 50-yard score. The touchdown came one play after FSU senior All-American Lamarcus Joyner was flagged for a dead-ball unsportsmanlike penalty.

And after Florida State caught a break when Auburn's Cody Parkey missed a short field goal, the unraveling continued on Winston's fumble at his own 27.

Marshall then did the honors himself on a four-yard TD to give the Tigers a stunning 21-3 lead. The touchdown came on third down, which was Auburn's specialty. In the first half alone, the Tigers converted 8 of 12 on third down. Florida State was just 2 of 8.

The Seminoles then seemed to be stopped again for a fifth consecutive three-and-out, but Fisher called for a fake punt in his own territory and Karlos Williams was able to convert.

Bryan Stork is overcome by emotion after Florida State defeats Auburn 34-31 to take the BCS National Championship game on Jan. 6, 2014 at the Rose Bowl in Pasadena, Calif. *Photo By: Glenn Beil/Democrat*

Winston then drove FSU the final 53 yards for the score. Freeman, who became the first Seminole back since Warrick Dunn in 1996 to gain 1,000 yards in a season, finished off the drive with a three-yard run, but the biggest play of the possession other than the fake punt was a Winston 21-yard scramble on third and 7.

It was a nice finish to a frustrating half for the Heisman Trophy winner, who had his worst statistical first half of the season by a wide margin. But even still, the Seminoles trailed by just 11 points and got the ball to start the third quarter.

While they didn't do anything on their first drive, the FSU offense did cut into the lead even more on its next possession, driving 60 yards to set up an Aguayo 41-yard field goal.

The Seminoles' defense seemed to right itself after halftime, keeping the Tigers scoreless on all three of their third-quarter drives. But Auburn punter Steven Clark continued to flip the field position, including downing a punt at the Seminole 4.

And Winston and the offense continued to struggle like it hadn't all season.

Auburn's defense was ranked No. 104 against the pass heading into the postseason, but through the first three quarters the Heisman Trophy winner and his talented cast of pass-catchers had just 120 yards on 11 of 25 passing.

Chad Abram leaps over an Auburn defender for a fourth-quarter touchdown as Florida State defeats Auburn 34-31 to take the BCS National Championship game on Jan. 6, 2014 at the Rose Bowl in Pasadena, Calif.
Photo By: Glenn Beil/Democrat

'NOLES PUNCH BACK, WIN TITLE

BY IRA SCHOFFEL

Above: P.J. Williams gets his leg whipped after making a big interception as Florida State defeats Auburn 34-31 to take the BCS National Championship game on Jan. 6, 2014.
Photo By: Glenn Beil/Democrat

Right: Jameis Winston, left, and Coach Jimbo Fisher head onto the field after Florida State defeats Auburn 34-31 to take the BCS National Championship game on Jan. 6, 2014.
Photo By: Glenn Beil/Democrat

PASADENA, Calif. — The great philosopher Mike Tyson once said, "Everybody has a plan until they get punched in the mouth."

OK, so maybe we can't rank Iron Mike up there with Descartes or Aristotle, but he had a point.

For four months, the Florida State football team ran roughshod over the ACC and a handful of non-conference opponents.

Of 13 games, 12 were blowouts ... and the other was decided early in the second half.

The question for the past month was whether the Seminoles could keep doing what they've been doing — passing the ball with incredible efficiency, running it for tough yards and playing smothering defense — after getting punched in the mouth by a team from the mighty Southeastern Conference.

On Jan. 6, 2014 in the BCS National Championship Game, No. 2 Auburn punched the Seminoles not once, not twice, but three times in the first half.

And guess what? The Seminoles punched back like only the No. 1 team can, rallying from an 18-point deficit to pull out a 34-31 victory and claim the school's third national championship. The great teams from 1993 and 1999 now have company.

FLORIDA STATE -VS- AUBURN

Jack Nicklaus, left, supports his grandson Nick O'Leary as Florida State defeats Auburn 34-31 to take the BCS National Championship game on Monday Jan. 6, 2014 at the Rose Bowl in Pasadena, Calif. *Photo By: Glenn Beil/Democrat*

That's right ... college football has a new national champion, and it comes from the ACC. The Southeastern Conference's streak of seven national titles is over.

For the first time in eight years, there were no chants of "S-E-C," "S-E-C" during the BCS trophy presentation. Just the hum of the war chant and the horns of the Florida State fight song from the Marching Chiefs.

The Seminoles were roughed up early, but they staggered the SEC's best with some brilliant second-half defensive adjustments.

After racking up 232 yards of offense in the first half, the Tigers gained just 45 in the third quarter. Then, FSU's offense got into the act.

Heisman Trophy-winning quarterback Jameis Winston, who took a flurry of haymakers in the first two quarters, was his old self down the stretch. He finished with 237 passing yards and two touchdowns with no interceptions. He also delivered some tough runs when the Seminoles needed them most.

FSU's wide receivers also came through after a tough first half. Rashad Greene and Kelvin Benjamin combined to catch 13 passes for 201 yards — with Benjamin catching the eventual game-winner with just 13 seconds remaining.

Everyone wondered how the Seminoles would handle a close game, how they would deal with adversity, but it was the battle-tested Tigers who seemed to wilt for much of the late going.

They only scored 10 points in the second half, and even after they reclaimed the lead late in the fourth quarter, they allowed FSU to drive 80 yards on seven plays in just 58 seconds to grab the win.

It was a completely different script from the regular season, when the Seminoles would often blow teams out in the first half and rest their starters in the second.

This time, the first half couldn't have gone much worse for the Seminoles.

The normally sure-handed Greene dropped a wide-open pass. Benjamin was non-existent in the first two quarters before coming to life in the second. And senior Kenny Shaw couldn't seem to get separation against Auburn's physical defensive backs.

The offensive line had more false starts in one game than in most months, and things weren't a whole lot better for the Seminoles' defense.

Ironically, Florida State did a very nice job against Auburn's powerful running game. It was the Tigers' passing attack that gave them fits early.

Call that a sucker punch, if you will.

But in the end, adversity just brought out the Seminoles' best.

Auburn showed it was a whole lot better than I and many others expected, but this Florida State team proved it was better than the rest of the world thought, too.

With Auburn defender Chris Davis, 11, hanging all over him, Kelvin Benjamin pulls in the game winning catch as Florida State defeats Auburn 34-31 to take the BCS National Championship.
Photo By: Glenn Beil/Democrat

Members of the Marching Chiefs get fired up as Florida State and Auburn meet for the BCS National Championship game on Jan. 6, 2014 at the Rose Bowl in Pasadena, Calif.
Photo By: Glenn Beil/Democrat

Florida State defeats Auburn 34-31 to take the BCS National Championship game on Monday Jan. 6, 2014. The hard-fought win earned FSU its third national title.
Photo By: Glenn Beil/Democrat

BOX SCORE

FLORIDA STATE 34, AUBURN 31

Florida St.	3	7	3	21	34
Auburn	7	14	0	10	31

First Quarter
FSU - Roberto Aguayo 35 FG, 9:53. *Drive: 9-59, 3.38.*
AUB - Tre Mason 12 pass from Nick Marshall (Cody Parkey kick), 3:07. *Drive: 6-25, 2:11.*

Second Quarter
AUB - Melvin Ray 50 pass from N. Marshall (C. Parkey kick), 13:48. *Drive: 3-85, 1:01.*
AUB - N. Marshall 4 run (C. Parkey kick), 5:01. *Drive: 6-27, 2:19.*
FSU - Devonta Freeman 3 run (R. Aguayo kick), 1:28. *Drive: 11-66, 3:33.*

Third Quarter
FSU - R. Aguayo 41 FG, 6:05. *Drive: 11-67, 5:30.*

Fourth Quarter
FSU - Chad Abram 11 pass from Jameis Winston (Aguayo kick), 10:55. *Drive: 5-56, 2:01.*
AUB - C. Parkey 22 FG, 4:42. *Drive: 13-69, 6:13.*
FSU - Levonte Whitfield, 65 kick return for TD, 4:31. *Drive: 13-100, 0:11.*
AUB - Tre Mason 37 run (C. Parkey kick), 1:19. *Drive: 8-75, 1:06.*
FSU - Kelvin Benjamin 2 pass from J. Winston (R. Aguayo kick), 0:13. *Drive: 7-80, 1:06.*

	FSU	AUB
First Downs	19	25
Rushes-Yards	31-148	53-232
Passing	237	217
Com-Att-Int	20-35-0	14-27-1
Return Yards	172	70
Punts-Avg.	6-42.8	6-43.2
Fumbles-Lost	2-1	2-0
Penalties-Yards	8-60	5-38
Time of Posession	26:19	33:41

Seminole fans at Madison Social in Tallahassee celebrate while watching the final minutes of the BCS Championship game.
Photo By: Michael Schwarz/Democrat